WRITING WHILE TRAVELIN(

WRITING WHILE TRAVELING ALL AROUND

Editor

Zennure KÖSEMAN

ISBN: 978-625-6968-43-1

First Edition: Kriter Yayınevi 2022 / İstanbul
Publisher Certificate No: 45353
First Edition, 176 p. 16 cm x 23,5 cm
Cover Design: Ahmed Baran
Layout: Kriter Yayınevi

Printing: Çözüm Baskı Merkezi Ticaret Limited Şirketi
Emniyetevleri Mahallesi Güvercin Sokak No:7/1 Kağıthane / İstanbul
Printing Press Certificate no: 49099

Contact Information:
Hobyar Mah. Cağaloğlu Yokuşu Sok. Fevzi Bey Han No: 21 Kat: 2 No: 5
Fatih / İstanbul

Tel: 0 212 527 31 89
info@kriteryayinevi.com
www.kriteryayinevi.com

WRITING WHILE TRAVELING ALL AROUND

Editor

Zennure KÖSEMAN

First Edition

2022 – İstanbul

KRİTER

Table of Contents

Introduction

Concerning writing during the process of traveling or expressing the feelings and emotions after ending a traveling is the basic interest of travel writers. Since the aim of travel writing is to state the different manners and customs in a place, thereby, readers can have information about different ways of living in various quarters. Hence, readers have the possibility to learn about different individuals in other places. Planning about traveling in a specific process helps readers to learn about the climate, historical background as well as regional qualities. This emphasizes travel writers' care about differences among regions.

After visiting all around, psychological and informative changes that places attribute to travel writers should also be considered. When a travel writer arrives at the place, first of all, she/he wants to be informed about the place. Then, she/he visits all around carefully and the traveler changes psychologically after being at the place. Traveling concurrently changes travelers emotionally because visiting a place is a source for a new writing about the setting freely. Having a specific reason while traveling either for enjoyment or for relaxing concurrently drives travelers to write about people living there, cultural values of that environment, historical information about the setting and psychological changes that the traveling causes.

Travel writing is a writing genre in which traveler describes the places she/he has visited and had different experiences while traveling. The traveler has a wide perspective to express about every detail of the place she/he visited. Travel writing can also have an interdisciplinary approach that combines historical, sociological and geographical considerations. The way people live, speak, cultural values they have and the historical period they live in are important to concern about. Thus, various interdisciplinary studies can be evaluated in travel writing.

Throughout interdisciplinary writing, several places can be visited and travelers by means of reading about the characteristics of that place keep in mind unforgettable aspects. They depict what they noticed there and how they are fascinated by the beauty of the environment. Travelers, thereby, remember their previous experiences they had in their previous years that became essential in their lives. Moreover, they convey their psychological changes in their writings so that the place and traveling activity had a significant role to influence inner worlds of visitors.

This book, *Writing While Travelling Around* will present several chapters about travel writing. It will present scholars' interpretations about their specific visits. It is concurrently considerable to state that several considerations while traveling would be a great subject for creative writing, because after traveling, it is time to express what kind of changes it created over individuals. Therefore, it is just the time to write freely in silence and produce new creative sources sticking in mind forever.

Several chapters in this book care for the transformational psychological evaluations. Writers express how the places visited and then written about reflected inner world transformations. To illustrate, Hasine Şen Karadeniz notes Robert Frost's poetic influence through explaining the Romantic footprints. Karadeniz conveys walking in the poetry of Robert Frost and implies how natural environment affect individuals. She emphasizes that Transcendentalist approach of Ralph Waldo Emerson and Henry David Thoreau should be reminded to state natural influence over individual psyches.

Meryem Ayan and Özlem Yılmaz comment on Eliot's "The Love Song of J. Alfred Prufrock" according to travel writing in between the lines. Since travel writing is mainly about experiences in journeys, then, comes travel writing on the views. They are traveler's subjective observations. What is significant is that those observations are all about the material and imaginary realms. As in Eliot's poetry, travel writing is a physical journey that gives information. The journey is in mind and the traveler travels in mind observations. The traveler fundamentally prefers to go towards his inside and find out his own self there. Hence, there is the mental traveling and the traveler wanders all around in his inner world. Therefore, Eliot's poetry has meaningful travel story in mind.

Zennure Köseman in her article notes about the sense dissatisfaction of individuals in their own settings for the means of traveling so that they look for other interesting places to visit as in Jack Kerouac's *On the Road*. Thereby, all individuals in the novel point out their psychological changes as they visit new places. They are all in a search for relaxing themselves due to experiencing the state of loneliness and isolation. What they care is to find new friendships in new environments. They are bored of the weariness of life due to hard work in daily life. They express their inner voice through listening to Jazz music as the Beat Generation did in *On the Road* to reflect their inner voice of loneliness. Thus, they expressed their thoughts, feelings, and emotions of their own lives.

As travels, trips, voyages reflect the effect of visited place on individual psyches, traveling becomes a great memoir in individual lives. It becomes impossible to forget those voyages as they deeply affect individual lives. To illustrate, Mevlüde Zengin, in her article, deals with Agatha Christie's *Come, Tell Me How You Live.* Christie also depicted abundantly the travels and expeditions of travelers and she noted the archeological explorations between 1930-1938 in Syria. Accordingly, she cares about her memoirs and writes about them in her target travel book. She conveys many implications and instances of Christie's own identity as an author. She has specific strategies, style and tone of writing. Finally, the book has fiction-like aspects and gives pleasure for readers while reading.

Another writer, Gül Koçsoy, considers Bartolomé de Las Casas' *A Short Account of the Destruction of the Indies* in the Light of Renaissance Humanism. A new outlook for Indies is given with Gül in a short account. Here, a Spanish bishop and missionary is explained to tell the atrocities done by the Spaniards to the Indigenous people. Even though he is a clergyman, he gives priority to humanist concerns in his short account. He, thereby, concerns about different places, cultures and languages. His work is ideological at the same time and documents slavery, defends the rights of them, as well as tells the situation to King Charles I of Spain by urging the pope to end the persecutions. Opposite to harsh exploitation and colonization, he mentions about a milder and more humane colonization. This indicates that under traveling account he has some other explanations.

In addition to the previous travel writers, there is Dilek Ünügür Çalışkan who cares about Jack Kerouac's *On the Road* from various perspectives. She expresses that there are inner and outer voyages into the contested spaces of cultural memory in Jack Kerouac's *On the Road.* In that book, she depicts that in addition to travel subject, the book is obsessed with sex, drug, and youth activity. She expresses the significance of inner and out voyages while traveling. She notes that in the novel, the music, Jazz music, is also important for individual psyches. This implies that, throughout the voyages, psychoanalysis of individuals is deeply influenced so that they regard themselves becoming new individuals. In this case, through the inner and outer voyages into the mental and geographical spaces of the cultural memory, individuals become new identities. Kerouac concurrently criticizes the new perspectives of behaviorism and psychoanalysis in his writing.

Aysel Deregözü concerns about the significance of travel writing in course books. In language teaching and learning, those books are considerable resources for teachers. Students encounter real life circumstances for their writing. There is the application of authentic material Deregözü underlines the significance of authentic writing in EFL classes and notes how travel writing is implemented in writing classes according to according the Process Approach Model She expresses that in a travel experience, there occurs brainstorming, planning, and structuring the ideas and notes in a meaningful way. Finally, the students write their ideas and structure the text they are going to write. They are going to write the draft version of the text in pairs or groups. In this case, travel writing is important in teaching classes

Finally, Elif Demir writes about Eric Newby's explorer-hero in the perspective of the subversion of the traditional image in *Round Ireland in Low Gear.* Demir notes that Newby with his wife Wanda travel to Ireland in *Round Ireland in Low Gear*. Newby concentrates on the couples and reflects that their voyage emphasizes the traditional image of the explorer-hero, because the cult of the explorer-hero reflects a national ambition, however, both Newby and Wanda travel for amusement. Demir also states about how women are historically disregarded from travel accounts as they are viewed as lacking strength. Therefore, weakness and failure are presented during their travel. However, a traditional explorer has a strong identity. This expresses that Newby and Wanda lack the prowess and prove to be anti-heroes travels. Therefore, humorous and self-ironizing attitudes transform the conventional aspect of heroism.

Walking in the Poetry of Robert Frost: a "Record Stride" in the Footprints of Romanticism and the Alleys of Modernism

Prof. Dr. Hasine Şen KARADENİZ

Abstract

This study explores mobility in Robert Frost's works defining his poetry as a buffer zone that fuses the Transcendentalist approach of Ralph Waldo Emerson and Henry David Thoreau with the modernist sensibility of Frost's contemporaries. The theme of walking in Frost's poetry is discussed under four subheadings: 1. "The Poem as a Walk" examines works that are constructed on an explicit walk-poem analogy. 2. "Walking in Nature and Poetic Vision" explores Frost's typical interest in rural traveling and presents it as a metaphor for the act of poetic composition. 3. Focusing on Frost's interest in science and technology, "The Walker and the Accelerated Pace of Technology" postulates that the road taken by the poet-wanderer in Frost's works bridges his Romantic worldview with modernist awareness. The last, fourth section of the argumentative part, "The Rhythm of the Walk/Poem: Human and Metrical Feet", discusses the link between the act of walking and rhythm in poetry claiming that Frost has left unique footprints in the track of conventional metric schemes.

Keywords: Walking, Romantic Worldview, Nature, Mobility, Robert Frost

Introduction

The Romantic interest in wandering in Nature and especially William Wordsworth's well-known fondness for walking, his tendency to view it as an externalized form of an inner search and to reflect this belief in his works are some of the major factors that have paved the way for a growingly increasing critical interest in the relationship between walking and poetry. Though the figure of the Romantic wanderer in Nature has been replaced by that of the modern *flaneur* who explores the urban terrain of the industrialized city, Robert Frost's poetry has been celebrated for continuing the tradition of Nature poetry amalgamating conventional poetic style with modernist awareness. Renowned works such as "The Road not Taken" and "Stopping by Woods on a Snowy Evening", as well as less popular poems such as "Boundless Moment", "An Encounter", "The Wood-Pile" and "Acquainted with the Night" reflect the perspective of Frost's conventional rural traveler. The motif of the trip to Nature and the description of plants, animals and scenes observed in the act of walking call to mind the simplicity of nineteenth century Fireside Poetry where the rumination on a natural object turns into a clear moral message stated generally in the familiar pattern of the iambic meter. Despite Frost's preference for the tried path of conventional metric schemes, the general sense of irresolution that governs his works and his tendency to perplex rather than instruct ally him strongly with his contemporaries too.

This chapter explores mobility in Robert Frost's poetry defining it as a buffer zone that fuses the Transcendentalist approach of nineteenth century American luminaries such as Ralph Waldo Emerson and Henry David Thoreau with the modernist sensibility of Frost's contemporaries. The theoretical background of the study is based on H.D. Thoreau's "Walking" (1862) and A.R. Ammons's "A Poem is a Walk" (1967) that establish a temporal bridge in the the debate on the relationship between walking and poetic production. The chapter focuses on the act of walking in Frost's poetry arguing that for the New England poet walking aims to stimulate thinking over moral categories rather than reaching a specific destination or asserting a definite idea. The theme of walking in Frost's poetry is discussed under four subheadings: 1. "The Poem as a Walk" examines *"To a Thinker"* and *"A Record Stride"*as works that are constructed on an explicit walk-poem analogy. 2. "Walking in Nature and Poetic Vision" explores Frost's typical interest in rural traveling in the poems "The Wood-Pile" and "Boundless Moment" and presents it as a metaphor for the act of poetic composition. 3. "The Walker and the Accelerated Pace of Technology" analyzes "Some Science Fiction", "An Encounter", "A Passing Glimpse" and

"Acquainted with the Night" and reaches the conclusion that the road taken by the poet-wanderer in Frost's works bridges the Romantic worldview with modernist awareness. The last, fourth section of the argumentative part, "The Rhythm of the Walk/Poem: Human and Metrical Feet", discusses the link between the act of walking and rhythm in poetry claiming that Frost has left unique footprints in the track of conventional metric schemes.

Walking and Poetry: Theoretical Perspectives

"The Poem is a Walk" by A. R. Ammons

In a lecture on the nature and function of poetry delivered to the International Poetry Forum in Pittsburg in 1967, A. R. Ammons defines the poem as a walk to highlight one of the poet's cardinal features, namely that s/he prefers "confusion over oversimplified clarity, meaninglessness to neat precise meaning, uselessness to overdirected usefulness" (15). This distinguishes his/her work from logical discourses that need the methodology of reason to establish clear formulations about the field(s) they explore. The poet does not totally discard this approach since "definition, rationality and structure" offer "ways of seeing" after all, yet his/her poetic sensitivity warns him/her that "they become prisons when they blank out other ways of seeing" (15). Ammons refers to Proteus, who occupies a minor position in the hierarchy of Olympus despite the fact that he is the god of *knowledge*, to show that "[d]efinite knowledge, knowledge specific and clear enough to be recognizable as knowledge, is... already limited into a minor view" (15). To differentiate the poem from the logical exposition and define it as a mode of writing that bridges inconsistencies to form an equally contradictory structure, Ammons identifies the poem as a walk and explains the analogy by listing four main similarities: "a walk involves the whole person; it is not reproducible: its shape occurs, unfolds: it has a motion characteristic of the walker" (18).

Ammons arrives at the definition that the poem is a walk, taking as a starting point the well accepted idea that a walk is the externalized form of an inner search. A detailed description of the four elements of Ammons' definition will be of use to elucidate the aptness of the metaphor he uses to define poetry. He starts with the all-inclusive and all-demanding aspect of both activities: "each makes use of the whole body, involvement is total, both mind and body...as with a walk, a poem is not simply a mental activity: it has body, rhythm, feeling, sound, and mind, conscious and subconscious. The pace at which a poet walks (and thinks) ... figures into the 'physiology' of the poem he writes" (16). The second resemblance the poet marks is that each walk is unique, as is every poem.

Even if a person takes the same route in his/her daily walks, each stroll is "unreproducible" as it is marked by the events that are witnessed that particular day and by the general mood of the walker. The next similarity spotted by Ammons underlines the power of good poetry to regenerate itself with each new reading and the ability of the poet to imprint his/her personal stamp while trying already tested poetic routes:

> The third resemblance between a poem and a walk is that each turns, one or more times, and eventually *re*turns. It's conceivable that a poem could take out and go through incident after incident without ever returning, merely ending in the poet's return to dust. But most poems and most walks return. (17-18)

The last resemblance in Ammons' list is linked to the rhythm of the walk/poem, a feature that emphasizes once more its singularity by accentuating the link between human and metrical feet. In addition to the listed qualities, "A Poem is a Walk" underlines "uselessness" as another common characteristic of walks/poems: "Only uselessness can allow the walk to be totally itself. ...[O]ur experience of poetry is least injured when we accept it as useless, meaningless, and nonrational" (19).

While attempting to FORMULATE his own theory of poetry, Ammons openly acknowledges the paramount impact of Coleridge's *Biographia Literaria* referring to his claim that poetry "reveals itself in the balance or reconciliation of opposite or discordant qualities" (13). Quoting also Wordsworth's "I wandered lonely as a cloud", he discloses the contribution of British Romantic poets for the germination of the walk-poem analogy. The reference to Wordsworth's famous poem is followed by the opening lines of two works by Robert Frost: "Now I out Walking" ("Away") and "Out walking in the frozen swamp one day" ("The Wood-Pile"). Ammons mentions the modern American poet along with his Romantic forefather to show that poets are fond of both walking and writing about walking in their works, yet this pairing is much more insightful, taking into account that Frost has always been hailed for his tribute to the spirit of Romanticism and Transcendentalism. While Ammons' text offers a serviceable theoretical frame for the study of his poems on walking, a brief evaluation of Romantic/Transcendentalist poetry is expedient to situate Frost within the tradition of American poetry in general and for specifying his interest in the theme of walking.

Transcendentalist Approaches: Ralph Waldo Emerson's "Apology" and Henry David Thoreau's "Walking"

One of the main concerns of the American poet since the colonial period has been the search for an authentic voice that would distinguish the poets of the new land from their predecessors from the mother country. It was only in the nineteenth century when Henry Wadsworth Longfellow, a member of a New England group known as the Fireside Poets (or Schoolroom Poets), got popular enough in both countries to be immortalized by a bust in the Poets' Corner at Westminster Abbey. In "On Trisyllabic Feet in Iambic Measure" (1819), William Cullen Bryant, another prominent member of the Fireside School, announces his conviction that American poetry should not be shackled by the rhythm of Neoclassical English verse, that "there may be departures from the accepted rules without marring the beauty of the structure" (61). His theory for the establishment of genuine American poetry is limited though to the departure from British metric patterns. In terms of content he postulates "infusion of moral sentiments to natural objects" or "the exhibition of analogies and correspondences... between the things of the moral and the natural world" (19) ("Lectures on Poetry", 1824), thus replicating the British Romantic notion of poetry. In his "Defence of Poetry" (1832), Longfellow makes a step further by presenting the treatment of national peculiarities such as American "scenery and climate, its historic recollections, its government, its various institutions" as prerequsite for founding a distinct voice in national poetry. Thus he urges his contemporaries to subordinate themselves to "the call of geography": "Describe a native landscape... Let us have no more sky-larks and nightingales... We wish to see... imagery of poetry which is a little more characteristic, as if drawn from nature and not from books" (75). Since "the call of geography" is a call for exploration, nineteenth century American poetry abounds in images of walking/wandering/loitering that define the poet as a mediator between Nature and the human world. Representative poems such as W.C. Bryant's "Thanatopsis", H.W. Longfellow's "Nature", O.W. Holmes's "The Chambered Nautilus", R. W. Emerson's "Each and All" define the poet as a figure who goes to Nature for an enlightening observation of a waterfowl, a chambered nautilus or a deserted nest and infuses it with a moral message.

Emerson's "The Apology" provides an eloquent illustration for the poet as a frequent visitor of Nature and for his attempt to justify himself for the "idle" hours he spends there in observation and rumination. The speaker-poet addresses the "labourious" members of society trying to explain to them the true nature of his work: "Think me not unkind and rude, / That I walk alone in grove and glen;/

I go to the god of the woods/ To fetch his word to men" (1-4). The poem goes on with two more stanzas that structurally repeat the opening four lines: a demand to be pardoned for the seemingly useless nature of the poet's work is followed by an explanation of its true character. Thus in the next stanza the speaker asks not to be "taxed" for "folding [his] arms beside the brook" because the reflection of each cloud "writes a letter into [his] book." Likewise, he does not want to be chided for bringing "idle" flowers from his walks in the woods because "every aster in [his] hand/ goes home loaded with a thought". The poem ends with a more convincing analogy: "One harvest from thy field/ Homeward brought the oxen strong;/ A second crop thine acres yield, / Which I gather in a song" (17-20). This stanza summarizes the essence of the regular trips of the Romantic bard to Nature: it is a huge classroom that inspires the poet and offers him scenes that can be translated to lessons on human morality.

Though Walt Whitman's messages derived from the contact with Nature are not as explicit as those of the aforementioned poets, his speaker's loitering in the woods finds embodiment in another song, "Song of Myself". The opening section of the work defines the poet as a walker who craves for a transcendental union with Nature: "I lean and loaf at my ease… observing a spear of summer grass/…I will go to the bank by the wood and become undisguised and naked, / I am mad for it to be in contact with me" (5-19). The image of the "laborious band" from Emerson's "Apology", the practical-minded people who cannot discern the internal value of the poet's efforts, turns in "Song of Myself" to that of an aggressive bird of prey: "The spotted hawk swoops by and accuses me, he complains of my gab and my loitering" (1331).

The acts of "walking alone", "loafing" and "loitering" described in these poems seem to bring to life a theory of walking postulated by H. D. Thoreau in his essay "Walking" (1862). In his eulogy for Thoreau, Emerson refers to his friend's "endless walks and miscellaneous studies" that offer "some new acquaintance with Nature (22). He underlines the importance of this act in his disciple's life adding that there was "nothing so important to him as his walk" and that he was always "ready for any excursion" (30). His affection for walking found expression in the importance he attached to the destinations and the routes he preferred: "He had many elegances of his own, whilst he scoffed at conventional elegance. Thus, he could not bear to hear the sound of his own steps, the grit of the gravel; and therefore never willingly walked in the road, but in the grass, on mountains and in woods" (1132). While Emerson views Thoreau's affection for walking as an extension of his desire for immersion into Nature, he also admits the importance of the relationship between the movement of the body and the work of the mind: "The length of his walk uniformly made the length of his writing. If shut up in the house, he did not write at all" (1133).

Reflecting a perspective reminding Thoreau's own life ideology, "Walking" (known also as "The Wild") has the scope and depth of a manifesto. The text presents this activity as an art of the highest rank. The narrator expresses his true admiration for people who "understood the art of Walking, that is, of taking walks - who had a genius, so to speak, for *sauntering*". He explains the origin of the word, stating that in the Middle Ages it was applied to people who roamed the countryside asking charity under the pretense of going to the Holy Land. Thus he defines the Saunterer as a Holy-Lander. The narrator provides another explanation suggesting that being derived from *sans terre* (without land or a home), the Saunterer is a person who has no particular home but feels at home everywhere (2079).

The true home for Thoreau's Saunterer is Nature, in tune with the principles of Transcendentalism he views the human being "as part and parcel of Nature, rather than a member of society" (2079). Thus, he becomes a spokesperson not only for the practitioners of the noble act of walking but a promoter of the value of "wildness" as the source of absolute freedom too. A walker is someone who takes the road after severing all his links with society: "if you have paid your debts, and made your will, and settled all your affairs, then you are ready for a walk" (2080). Thus the art of walking demands both physical and mental involvement. Thoreau's hero views detachment from social concerns as cardinal because he believes that a person cannot become part of Nature as long as he carries in his mind the burden of civilization. While in "Civil Disobedience" Thoreau promotes resistance to communal restraints, in "Walking" he proposes walking as a temporary escape from societal control.

As far as the road, the walker's major requisite, is concerned, Thoreau postulates the fresh, untried path or the one that has been tried and forgotten because a good walker is stimulated not by the drive to reach a known destination but by the mystery of where the new path leads to. As the nest of "wildness", "west" is his favourite direction, while east is linked in his mind with the culture and habits of the "old" continent. His preference to move west is in tune with the doctrine of Manifest Destiny, yet for him the unexplored American wilderness is a territory to walk through, not a source to be distributed among business-minded newcomers. Thoreau's Saunterer is hostile to private property as fences, walls and hedges divide "God's Earth" to "pleasure gounds" with limited use and obstruct the walker's freedom to move in the direction he pleases (2085).

Thoreau's walker is ostensibly a poet who views wandering as a prelude to the act of poetic production. He illustrates this referring to Wordsworth, the embodiment of the figure of the poet as a walker: "When a traveler asked Wordsworth's servant to show him her master's study, she answered, "Here is his library, but his study is out of doors" (2081). Thoreau provides a more detailed explanation of the relationship between physical and mental paths in "Walden", in the section where he explains why he left the woods:

> I left the woods for as good reason as I went there… It is remarkable how easily and insensibly we fall into a particular route, and make a beaten track for ourselves. I had not lived there a week before my feet wore a path from my door to the pondside; and though it is five or six years since I trod it, it is quite distinct. It is true, I fear, that others may have fallen into it, and so helped to keep it open. The surface of the earth is soft and impressible by the feet of men; and so with the paths which the mind travels. How worn and dusty, then, must be the highways of the world, how deep the ruts of tradition and conformity! (236)

Evaluating poets such as Chaucer, Milton and Shakespeare, the narrator of "Walking" defines them as too civilized, too tamed. While they represent the paths of "tradition and conformity", it is Greek mythology that embodies the spirit of wildness the Saunterer treasures so much. Applying the nature-culture, wildness-domestication, freedom-control dichotomies to the field of art, Thoreau postulates that poetry has the potential to express wild vigor even when it follows the track of tradition.

With his exceptional ability to bridge the modernist sensibility of his contemporaries with the conventional style of his Romantic predecessors, Frost's works offer a powerful illustration for the idea of poetry disclosed in "Walking". The travelers in familiar works such as "The Road not Taken" and "Stopping by Woods on a Snowy Evening" can easily be defined as saunterers in Thoreau's terms yet this study focuses on less known works that either openly establish the walk-poem, walking-thinking analogies or discuss the act of walking as a metaphor for poetic creation or life.

The Act of Walking in the Poetry of Robert Frost

Besides signaling a steady interest in the theme of walking, "The Road not Taken", one of Frost's most widely quoted poems, reveals his exceptional ability to use seemingly accessible images and situations to trigger thoughts about the complexity of human existence. The resistance to closure can be defined as the main feature that unites different categories of poems that explore the relationship between walking, thinking and poetry. Frost is known mainly for his works about lonely travelers in dark winter woods, yet he has a number of poems that describe walking with a companion too. Equating the acts of "walking" to that of "talking", they present the shared promenade as a method of expanding the walker's expertise in "country things" ("The Black Cottage"), of questioning the validity of his own ideas or the worldview of his interlocutor ("Blueberries") or as an expression merely of the human need for interaction ("A Time to Talk"). Another exception is the group of poems that deal with urban travelling and the impact of technology and science on the perception of the walker/poet.

Frost's preoccupation with mobility has been marked by a number of critics too. In "Motion in Stevens and Frost" G. Gabrielle Starr asserts that the walk is used by Frost as a structuring device and as a "model for memory" (90). The scholar discusses how "Directive" captures this "intimate linkeage between motion and memory" by focusing on the images of decay that invite the speaker to "a guided walk back into childhood" (91). Tracing Frost's personal geographical mobility and discussing its impact on his poetry, Candice Lemaire's "The Constant Traveler: Staging Mobility in the Poetry of Robert Frost" provides an insightful analysis of poems such as "Record Stride", "Away" and "A Leaf-Treader" in the light of the concept of "extravagance", a term Frost explained to the students of Dartmouth College in 1962, while he was "barding about", as the poet himself referred to the numerous readings and talks he gave in colleges. Lemaire discusses the etymology of the term "extravagance" and applies it to Frost's own poetry:

> More than a mere expression of American extravagance (understood as "eccentricity", "excess", or "spectacular flamboyance"), Frost's poetry can be seen as a product of an extreme "extra-vagance", understood as a poetry of wandering rather than of wondering. Frost's poetical "extra-vagance" is his constant wandering beyond his bounds, within and beyond the geographical limits of his territory (as the Latin etymology of "extravagance" justifies: *extra-vagari*, to wander outside, to exceed the bounds of a space). (1)

Frost's "extra-vagance" can surely be linked to his interest in the Romantic tradition and its focus on Nature. The New England poet has written a significant amount of poems that discuss the relationship between walking in Nature and the act of writing poetry. "Time Out", for example, presents the time spent "out" as a period of active contemplative reading since nature is "a text, albeit done in plant" that offers a "a moment to reflect". This is clearly the perspective of Fireside Poetry, yet in contrast to his nineteenth century predecessors, Frost suspends the moment of reflection into a fleeting instant of clarification that provides only "a momentary stay against confusion" as the poet formulates poetry in "The Figure a Poem Makes". This approach is valid for Frost's works that situate the walker in the less typical terrain of the city or discuss how he reads the signs of scientific and technological progress too. The first two poems discussed in this chapter ("To a Thinker" and "A Record Stride") illustrate the idea of the poem as a walk explicated by A.R. Ammons in "The Poem is a Walk."

The Poem as a Walk: "To a Thinker" and "A Record Stride"

"To a Thinker" is one of Frost's works where poetry is defined through explicit walking/thinking imagery. The poem is written in the form of a dramatic monologue from the perspective of a "bard" who addresses an unnamed companion ("you") disclosing to him his notion of poerty: "The last step taken found your left/ Decidedly upon the left./ One more would throw you on the right./ Another still-you see your plight./ You call this thinking, but it's walking" (1-5). The opening lines imply a debate about the nature of the activity the speaker is engaged in. While the silent companion names it constructively as "thinking", the speaker opposes him by definig his pastime humbly as "walking" and then reducing its status to that of "only rocking", and even "weaving like a stabled horse" (6-7). Since the speaker discloses his identity in the last line, the poem acquires the form of a riddle about his occupation. While "weaving" is not an appropriate activity for a stabled horse, combined with the list of movements in the ensuing lines, it defines him as someone who deals with poetic activity:

> From force to matter and back to force,
> From form to content and back to form,
> From norm to crazy and back to norm,
> From bound to free and back to bound,
> From sound to sense and back to sound.
> So back and forth. (8-13)

The repetitive pattern "from...to...and back to" clearly envisions the poet as a walker who has to wear many mental paths to arrive at a desired verbal destination. Moving constantly between conflicting notions, the speaker-poet views himself as a person to whom "things come in pairs" (14). The "form-content", "bound-free", and "sound-sense" dualities are eloquent enough to unveil his vocation as a "weaver" of poems. Read retrospectively, the term "force" in the pair "force- [subject]matter" materializes as what E.A. Poe had defined as the "effect" of any poetic construct in "The Philosophy of Composition". The sense of disorientation caused in the tour from "norm" to "crazy" points to another vital aspect of the journey of versification. The bard should observe existing poetic norms, he should be "bound" to tradition to be accepted into the guild of wordsmiths, yet he should be "crazy", innovative and free enough to establish his genuine poetic voice. Introducing other dualities such as "democracy-dictatorship", "reformer-reformed", "To a Thinker" defines the ultimate goal of the poem/walk as establishing a middle ground without opting for a specific meaning/destination.

"A Record Stride" develops the walk-poem analogy by clarifying the nature of the poet's seemingly aimless promenades as an attempt to "record" the experiences he had witnessed or been involved in. The work is written from the perspective of an elderly bard who projects his thoughts to "a pair of shoes" that had accompanied him in his "record stride". These "old rivals" that "once kept surpassing each other" (6-7) are now engaged in a debate about "who is too old to go walking" (11). The fact that the question is uttered "with too stress on the who" (12) reveals that the speaker is actually concerned with his own age and employs his last creative potential to evaluate his career.

The usage on the term "extra-vagant" for the presentation of the "past-active shoes" is significant, having in mind the function of this word in Frost's definition of poetry: "And poetry is a sort of extravagance, in many ways. It's something that people wonder about. What's the need of it? And the answer is, no need - not particularly" ("Extravagance", 21). Candice Lemaire refers to Jeffrey S. Cramer's explanation that "Frost hyphenated the word "extra-vagant" in the fourth stanza to either act on the metrical length of the line or to allude to Thoreau who also hyphenated the word in *Walden*, reinforcing once more the feature of "extra-vagance" they share" (3). Viewing the extravagance of his activity as a verification for a fruitful career, the elderly poet is proud to devote his "record stride of stretch" (32) to his "museum and muse" (30). The elusive alliterative phrase finds explanation in the final lines of the poem where the speaker asks forgiveness for his ecstatic tone: "And I ask all to try to forgive me/ For being as overelated/ As if I had measured the country/ And got the United States stated" (33-36).

The speaker-poet of Frost's works is generally a lonely walker who explores the terrain of rural New England and the aging bard in "A Record Stride" is cautious to be misunderstood as overrating his poetic talent. From that point of view the work can be interpreted as a confession of Robert Frost himself as a representative American poet who has partially "stated" the United States by "measuring" the geography of New England in the rhythmic measures of "old" England.

Walking in Nature and Poetic Vision: "The Wood-Pile"* and *"Boundless Moment"

"The Wood-Pile" is a typical nature poem describing the figure of a hesitant traveler who explores the unconventional beauty of a frozen pond. Though structured as a narrative work, the focus on "walking" as a central event elevates strolling to the rank of an activity with a dramatic power: "Out walking in the frozen swamp one gray day/ I paused and said, 'I will turn back from here./ No, I will go on farther—and we shall see'" (1-3). These opening lines establish the speaker as a contemplative though irresolute stroller who does not have a specific goal in his mind. This turns the act of walking, as marked by Crowley, into an "epitome of Frost's conviction that 'calculation is usually no part in the first step of any walk'". Bruce Meyer suggests that the speaker "is on a journey not simply through the woods, but through his own epistemology" too and interprets the act of walking as a metaphor for the discovery of the unexpected and the ways in which that discovery is comprehended" (257). As "The Wood-Pile" chronicles both a physical journey and the march of thoughts in the traveler's mind, the poem can be read as a report of the poetic activity itself.

The speaker reminds the figure of the artist described in "The Figure a Poem Makes" where Frosts explains the most important difference between scholars and artists as the method through which they obtain knowledge: Scholars acquire knowledge with "conscientious thoroughness along projected lines of logic" while poets "stick to nothing deliberately, but let what will stick to them like burrs where they walk in the fields" (1116). The burrs of inquisitiveness that arrest the walker in this poem are a cautious bird and a neat pile of wood, two images that provoke equivocal thoughts about the relationship between nature and civilization.

The opening words of the poem ("Out walking in") deserves special attention as they introduce the main activity the speaker is engaged in, "walking", and the ambiguous direction of his movement indicated by the contradictory prepositions "out" and "in": "the phrase is so solidly idiomatic, so much a mode of common speech, that all its powers of suggestion (namely, the juxtaposition of externality and internality) are playfully hidden, buried beneath the plainness of the words themselves" (Crowley). Thus from the very first step/line, walking as a physical activity is linked to the march of the speaker's thoughts. The nature of the experiences reported in the opening lines strengthens the speaker's tendency to constantly shift from externality to internality. The outward excursion described in the first line is immediately interrupted by a pause that gives birth to an internal monologue about "turning back", back home, back to the predictable rhythm of daily obligations. This idea is repudiated by the decision "to go on father" into the uncharted realm of the wilderness. It is worth noting that Ammons quotes the three opening lines of this work to illustrate the third resemblance between a walk and a poem, namely the fact "that each turns, one or more times, and eventually *re*turns" (17). Marking that there is no return in this poem and that it is only implied, Ammons comments on its function: "But the turns and returns or implied returns give shape to the walk and to the poem. With the first step, the number of shapes the walk might take is infinite, but then the walk begins to 'define' itself as it goes along, though freedom remains total with each step: any tempting side road can be turned into on impulse, or any wild patch of woods can be explored" (17).

In addition to the outward-inward, physical-mental, movement-stasis, home-nature dichotomies invoked by the opening lines of the poem, the third line introduces the personal-communal perspective by the shift of the pronoun "I" to "we": "No, I will go on farther—and we shall see" (3). Crowley links this change to the dual character of the speaker: "He has become at once his own reassuring guide and cautious initiate. And since it is the "we" who shall see, what is to be discovered will be informed by both". In her detailed reading of the poem Mary K. Ruby notes that "'we shall see' is a common twist of language for a simple, plainspoken person, but in this poem it implies that the speaker, though he walks alone, thinks of himself as being bound to some greater being—perhaps nature or God" (252). He needs reassurance by a force within or without because he has to tame the fears and anxieties caused by the unpredictable winter landscape because he has taken the risk of walking upon a frozen pond. The certitude expressed in the phrase "The hard snow held me" (4) discloses the speaker's belief that the strange environment instills in him a sense of security offered only by a well-known and repeatedly tested terrain. Yet the subordinate clause of the same sentence dilutes the idea of nature's safety and introduces solid examples of danger: The ice forms a substantial platform for the walker "save where now and then/ One foot went through" (4-5).

Robert Faggon concentrates rather on the verb "see" in the phrase "we shall see" questioning whether it is used literally or colloquially, as in "see what will happen". This remark is enlightening having in mind the difference between the acts of *seeing* and *looking* in relation to the process of ruminative walking. In a dissertation about Thoreau's "Walking", Camila Alvares Pasquetti defines *looking* as the characteristic activity of the traveler referring to Sergio Cardoso's theoretical observations on the two modes of visual response to reality:

> For the one who sees, nothing is strange, the world is plain and each part of it composes the whole. The act of looking, however, carries an intentional connotation: the subject who looks has the power and responsibility of interfering with the object that is being regarded. The look, therefore, is not passive; one moves forward instigated by the curiosity to "see again, " or to "see the new" (348). ...The eye of the traveler is the eye which moves in space and time in search for the strange, for what is unfamiliar, that is, for what is not stable or ordered – it is the eye which looks for the "other" and for the "new." (7-8)

The walker in "The Wood-Pile" is surely engaged in looking rather than seeing yet what he looks at is not surprising nor new. His attention is initially arrested by the trees that surround him because their uniformity enhances his sense of insecurity in the atmosphere of the winter landscape: "The view was all in lines/ Straight up and down of tall slim trees/ Too much alike to mark or name a place by/ So as to say for certain I was here/Or somewhere else" (5-9). Walking in the winter wood does not prove to be safe nor rewarding since the surrounding view of similar trees enveloped in the uniformity of whiteness dissolves all notions of goal and direction. The speaker's only notion of certainty is linked to the idea that he is "just far from home" (9):

> If 'just' points up the severe, even terrifying, limits of his knowledge at this point of the process, it also simultaneously emphasizes his diminished anxiety regarding those limits. The word at once generates a sense of terror and dispels it. The effect is almost that the terrors of "homelessness, " of being lost in undifferentiated space, comprise a condition the speaker has known before and finds so persistent and multifarious as to demand his constant re-engagement. (Crowley)

The tendency to postpone the moment of turning back home, to the human-made world of control, predictability and safety, indicates that the speaker shares the itch for the wandering experience described by H.D. Thoreau in "Walking":

> Hope and the future for me are not in lawns and cultivated fields, not in towns and cities, but in the impervious and quaking swamps.... When I would recreate myself, I seek the darkest woods the thickest and most interminable and, to the citizen, most dismal, swamp. I enter a swamp as a

> sacred place, *a sanctum sanctorum*. There is the strength, the marrow, of Nature. The wildwood covers the virgin mould, and the same soil is good for men and for trees.... A township where one primitive forest waves above while another primitive forest rots below - such a town is fitted to raise not only corn and potatoes, but poets and philosophers for the coming ages. (2090-91)

The walker in "The Wood-Pile", just like Thoreau's saunterer, is not tempted merely by the pictorial aspects of Nature. The frozen pond, as one of her deepest and wildest facets, urges him through the power of a belief expressed in "Walking" in the maxim that "the most alive is the wildest" (2090).

The speaker's seemingly uneventful journey in the unfathomable depth of the wilderness is cheered by the sight of a small bird and the confrontation with this tiny feathered friend unleashes a new flood of speculations about the relationship between the human being and nature: "A small bird flew before me. He was careful/ To put a tree between us when he lighted, / And say no word to tell me who he was/ Who was so foolish as to think what *he* thought" (10-13). After the plain appearance of the same looking trees, the entrance of the bird brings in a certain confusion to the scene but the atmosphere of complexity is created through the awkward diction of the bird's description rather than the animal itself. As the bird is personified it is designated with the personal pronoun "he" and endowed with the capacity to ruminate about the human visitor. The bird is cautious enough to perch on a safe distance after putting the barrier of a tree between itself and the visitor. Its suspicious approach is enhanced by the fact that it says "no word" to tell the visitor "who he was". The repetition of the pronoun "he" as a specifier of the undisclosed performer of the activity of thinking in the next line (the bird and/or the speaker), turns this part of the poem almost into a riddle that recreates on a verbal level the "lines" of identical trees that fail to function as sign posts. Pritchard defines these two lines as the most playful part of the poem because "the monosyllabic tongue-twisting aspect of these lines is effective in mixing up the reader: who is more 'foolish, ' man or bird, and how on earth can one tell?" Despite the apparent friendliness of the speaker and his tendency to view the bird in human terms, he actually projects his own thought process to the denizen of the wood and presents himself from its perspective: "He thought that I was after him for a feather—/The white one in his tail; like one who takes/ Everything said as personal to himself./ One flight out sideways would have undeceived him" (14-17).

The brief tension introduced with the confrontation with the fearing bird ends with the sudden shift in the speaker's interest to a pile of wood, the main signpost in the uncharted ground of the winter forest: "And then there was a pile of wood for which/ I forgot him and let his little fear/ Carry him off the way I might have gone, / Without so much as wishing him good-night" (18-21). The shift of the speaker's attention from the bird to the wood-pile solidifies the impression that he is a person who can easily change the goal of his pursuit. In the opening lines of the poem he easily disclaims the decision to turn back preferring to continue his walk. The act of giving up the bird and focusing on a pile of wood indicates that the speaker is a pensive wanderer who follows whatever path his curiosity and imagination choose. Actually it is the bird that directs his attention to the woodpile as "he went behind it to make his last stand" (22). The sight of the deserted wood-pile prolongs the pause in the speaker's walk, hence the speed of its description slows down to monitor minutest details ranging from its physical characteristics to its history:

> It was a cord of maple, cut and split
> And piled—and measured, four by four by eight.
> And not another like it could I see.
> No runner tracks in this year's snow looped near it.
> And it was older sure than this year's cutting,
> Or even last year's or the year's before.
> The wood was gray and the bark warping off it
> And the pile somewhat sunken. Clematis
> Had wound strings round and round it like a bundle. (23-26)

Stated in Faggen's terms, the speaker sees in the monumental wood-pile an "ambiguous evidence of order and cultivation that does not yield simple revelations". Someone has cut maple wood, arranged it in a perfect pile and left it useless in the woods. Besides affording the pleasure of a walk in the woods, the speaker is obviously someone who can tell the age of cut wood just by casual inspection. Marking that it is "gray" and that the "bark is warping off" he reaches the conclusion that it is not freshly cut. Furthermore, he notices that the pile is "somewhat sunken", it has stayed there long enough to shrink into the ground and to be covered by strings of clematis. This expertise on cut wood is a faculty described in the title of another poem by Frost as "[t]he need of being versed in country things". As a person who observes the landscape from the perspective of a countryman who is aware of his dependence on natural forces, the speaker is practical enough to specify the measurements of the pile as "four by four by eight". His competence in country things is never divorced from a strong disposition for philosophical rumination either, as Crowley marks in the discussion of Frost's numerical precision:

> What Frost has done in "making his count" of the woodpile's dimensions is to carry those numbers into time, and in doing so he has transformed the straightness and angularity of the landscape into curves, into roundness and sphericity. This transformation is initially hinted at, I think, in the multiple suggestiveness of "cord, " which is not only the specific name given to 128 cubic feet of fuel wood but, here, a pun on the mathematical term denoting a straight line which joins two points on an arc or curve. The change wrought in the speaker's perception of the scene is a brilliant poetic realization of Frost's conviction that "We are what we are by elimination and by deflection from the straight line."

Further inspection of the woodpile shows that on one side it is propped by "a tree/ *still growing*", while on the other side it is supported by "a stake and prop, /these latter *about to fall*" (32-34, emphasis mine). While the image of the clematis wrapping the wood-pile implies cohabitation, thus mutual aid, these lines contrast the natural and the human-made suggesting the essential vitality of nature and the fragility of human constructs. From the pile of wood, the speaker's attention shifts to the anonymous stranger who had discarded it after wasting time and energy to cut and pile it:

> I thought that only
> Someone who lived in turning to fresh tasks
> Could so forget his handiwork on which
> He spent himself, the labor of his ax,
> And leave it there far from a useful fireplace
> With the slow smokeless burning of decay. (35-40)

Despite the fact that the wood-pile is presented in terms of wastefulness, Ruby suggest that "[i]n the end, the effort is not presented as having been wasted at all, since the decaying wood is expending its energy back into the frozen swamp—into the tree at whose base it sits. Thus, the axeman's effort does not result in personal gain, but it benefits nature" (254). This marks a shift in the speaker's notion of what "home" is. In the opening lines, being "far from home" raises certain fears because the fragility of the ice does not offer a stable ground to rest upon. At the end of the poem the frozen swamp turns into a huge fireplace, the conventional symbol of domestic tranquility. The description of the fireside as "useful" contrasts with the "wasteful" energy invested in the pile of wood. Combined with the targetless stroll of the speaker, the "usefull-useless" dichotomy reminds the central feature of the walk/poem defined by Ammons as "uselessness". Thus, having in mind Frost's own notion of "extravagance", the poem can be read as a metaphor for the act of poetic creation.

"A Boundless Moment" can be approached from a similar perspective as the poem reports a brief instance from the walking experience of an unnamed speaker ("I") and his unnamed companion ("he") when their journey is suddenly interrupted by the sight of something "pale" (2) in the distance. At the end of the poem the travelers "move on" (11) having identified it as a "a young beech clinging to its last year's leaves" (12). Frost manages to report this casual rural occurrence as a highly suspenseful experience and presents it as a "boundless moment" of visual (mis)perception. The tension is caused not merely by the mysterious nature of the distant object but also by the conflict between the two walkers. While the speaker's companion is "ready to believe the most" (4), namely that it is a "ghost", the speaker announces self-confidently that it is a flower, "the Paradise-in-Bloom" (5). Yet he immediately disowns his own perception remembering that the season ("March") is unlikely for "such white luxirience of May" (8). The moment of clarification, reported in the third stanza of the poem, discloses that perception can be deceptive, and that people can manipulate other people's perceptions too:

> We stood a moment so, in a strange world,
> Myself as one his own pretence deceives;
> And then I said the truth (and we moved on).
> A young beech clinging to its last year's leaves. (9-12)

Thus the "boundless moment" ceases as the atmosphere of the "strange world" (of the speaker's imagination and his companion's superstitions) dissolves with the declaration of "truth". Restored to the reality of the early spring maple wood, the two men resume their walk but the correctness of their last negotiated perception remains uncertain. The "boundless moment" experienced by them evokes the idea of the "momentary stay against confusion," the brief moment of clarification Frost envisions as the goal of poetry.

The Walker and the Accelerated Pace of Technology: "Some Science Fiction", "An Encounter", "A Passing Glimpse" and "Acquainted with the Night"

Though nature and the rural life of New Englanders are the major themes of Frost's poetry, he has a number of works that demonstrate deep concern with scientific discoveries and the rapid development of technologies too. Emblematic poems such as "Fire and Ice", "Why Wait for Science" and "Bursting Rupture" provide a convincing example for Frost's awareness that the new age transformed by the advent of the car, the airplane, the telephone and the fear of the atomic bomb calls for new poetic responses. Ezra Pound's "Hugh Selwyn Mauberley" clarifies that "the age demanded an image/ Of its accelerated grimace" (24-25), that it required "prose kinema, not, not assuredly, alabaster/ Or the sculpture of rhyme" (35-36). Poems by Frost such as "Some Science Fiction", "An Encounter", "A Passing Glimpse" and "Acquainted with the Night" exploit the image of walking to show how the accelerated speed of contemporary life transforms the perception of reality and calls for new poetic diction. The tone of ambiguity characteristic of Frost's nature works dominates his poems on science, technology and urban life too. Any final assertion related to the intrusion of technology into the wilderness or its transformative impact on poetic imagination remain "suspended rather than being asserted" as Macgowain states to describe the poet's resistance to neat conclusions (39).

"Some Science Fiction" explores the poem-walk analogy by juxtaposing the figure of the speaker-poet to that of the "headlong human race" (4), a collective term designating the speaker's contemporaries who are obsessed with scientific and technological progress. Frost's criticism is directed not at science and technology in general, he disclaims those who "get more nuclear/ and more bigoted in reliance/ on the gospel of modern science" (14-16). Presenting the bard as a pedestrian who walks too slow to catch up with the accelerated pace of science, the work underlines social engagement and philosophical depth as essential features of the artist. The members of the hasty community that disregards the moral dimensions of scientific advancement nevertheless "mind" the poet's decision to "stay back behind" (5-6). As a person who is inclined "to take life at a walk/ in philosophic talk" (6-8), they do not view him as a rival nor a serious enemy, and "only smile/ at how slow [he does] a mile" (9-10). Despite this denigrating approach the speaker is aware of his own superiority:

> For them my loitering around
> At less than the speed of sound
> Or even the speed of light
> Won't seem unheretical quite. (17-20)

The twisted logic of the last line provides a solid clue for the nature of the speaker's power. As a master of words, he can challenge the "headlong human race" with crafty lines born by the insightful and provocative thoughts of his seemingly purposeless sauntering. Presenting ironically the possibility to banish the poet to a "penal colony… on the moon" (21-22) as "some science fiction", as the title of the poem informs, Frost expresses his hostility to scientific and technological progress divorced from moral incentive. On a more general level, the poet's attempt to justify his own "loitering" turns the poem into an act of formal defense reminding Emerson's "Apology" discussed above.

The walk in "An Encounter" is interrupted by rumination about the impacts of technology too. An inquisitive speaker-walker has "left the road [he]knew" (7) to find himself "half boring through, half climbing through/ a swamp of cedar" (4-5). The moment he stops and looks "up toward heaven" his attention is arrested by a telephone post, "a resurrected tree, / a tree that had been down and raised again" (11-12). The speaker's approach to this sign of technological progress is more ambivalent than his open hostility to the tendency "to get more neucler" in the previous poem. The tree that has been granted a second life is personified and presented in equal terms with the walker: "He had halted too, / as if for fear of treading upon [the rambler]" (14-15). The ensuing dialogue demonstrates one of Frost's favourite techniques: projecting the speaker's thoughts to the inanimate objects he encounters in his regular strolls. Thus the resurrected tree that carries news "from men to men" (18) is paradoxically "not off for anywhere at all" (22) and just like the speaker who digresses from the familiar road, the resurrected tree "wander[s] out of beaten ways" (23). Thus the final line of the poem, "half looking for the orchid Calypso" (24) can be attributed to both the speaker and the articulate tree. Though imbued with notes of longing for a lost "orchid Calypso", the process of "*half* looking" in the closing verse demonstrates that the speaker is torn apart between the impulse to follow the beaten track and the temptation to leave it.

While many of the travelers of Frost's poems are walkers, "A Passing Glimpse" discusses the advantages and disadvantages of observing the world from a "passing car" or a "train". While walking offers the opportunity to stop and scrutinize an object of interest – be it a wood-pile, a telephone pole, a bird or a tree– the speed of a vehicle guarantees only a momentary, "passing glimpse": "I often see flowers from a passing car/ That are gone before I can tell what they are" (1-2). Driven by the impulse of the walker within him, the speaker wants "to get out of the train and go back/ to see what they were beside the track" (3-4). The poem goes on with the realization that the observation of the world from a moving car or a train obstructs the passenger's vision and results in doubts about the accuracy of representation:

> I name all the flowers I am sure they weren't:
> Not firewood loving where woods have burnt-
> Not bluebells gracing a tunnel mouth-
> Not lupine living on sand and drouth. (5-8)

The speaker's preoccupation with flowers shows that he is actually a lover of nature and travelling by car or train revives the memory of old walking experiences. At this point the passenger's concern with the warting effect of the vehicle's speed shifts to an implicit criticism of industrialization and mechanization: Fireweed do not grow in areas of burnt woods as the flower's name ironically implies; bluebells do not decorate tunnel mouths but lush meadows, lupine likewise do not "live on sand and drouth" but on fertile ground. These speculations disclose the speaker's expertise in plants and imply a deep awareness of the destructive effect of technological progress. The poem nevertheless does not condemn it. The complaint in the opening lines about the difficulty of identifying flowers from a moving car turns into a more affirmative statement: "Heaven gives its glimses only to those/ not in position to look too close" (11-12). Thus the idea of limitation as a product of accelerated speed acquires general proportions and turns into a declaration of the power of the poet's insightfulness.

"Acquainted with the Night" is one of Frost's few poems where the act of walking takes place on a distinctly urban terrain: a despondent flaneur wanders in the "saddest city lane" (5), reporting images of despair and descent reminding the scenes recorded by J. Alfred Prufrock in his epic stroll in "half deserted streets... that follow like a tedious argument" (4-8). Like Eliot's hero, the speaker is a lonely individual with heightened poetic sensibility but in contrast to Prufrock, whose wandering in the dismal city streets is motivated by a desire to belong to a sophisticated society of women "talking about Michelangelo" (14), Frost's walker does not even feel the urge to relate to the city: "I have looked down the saddest city lane./ I have passed by the watchman on his beat/ And dropped my eyes, unwilling to explain" (4-6). The sudden halt in the next line "I have stood still and stopped the sound of feet" (7), enhanced by its strong alliterative pattern, creates tension and anticipates an event that will trigger the speaker's urge to relate to and "explain" but his description of the "interrupted cry" (8) only reveals an attempt to justify his disengagement: the cry comes from "far away", from "houses from another street" (9) and it does not aim to "call [him]back or say good-by" (10). The sense of tediousness achieved with the cyclic nature of the to and fro movement ("I have walked out in rain – and back in rain" (2)) is enhances with the structure of the poem too. Starting and ending with the same line ("I have been acquainted with the night"), the poem designates a fruitless journey that escalates the walker's sense of despair. Having "outwalked the farthest city light" (3), he seems to have exhausted his desire to move ahead.

This poem resembles in mood works with typical rurarl settings such as "Stopping by Woods on a Snowy Evening" and "Good Hours". Both poems present a traveler who speculates on the beauty and peacefulness of a winter evening. The title of the latter poem implies, ironically, the ritual practice of "keeping good hours" (going to bed early) in rural areas. Nevertheless, the speaker is a reclusive person who does not fit into the general pattern of village life preferring a meditative walk along the line of silent cottages: "I had for my winter evening walk -/ No one at all with whom to talk" (1-2). The usage of the terms "walk" and "talk" as rhyming words accentuates the intrinsic relationship between the two acts. Deprived of a companion, the speaker records his physical movement as an inward journey, as a meditation on self-imposed loneliness and the final solitude brought by death. Despite the difference of setting, the urban walker in "Acquainted with the Night" and the rural travelers in "Stopping by Woods on a Snowy Evenening" and "Good Hours" are united by the centrality of the images of darkness and night that present walking as a metaphor for human life. This common theme demonstrates Frost's skill in addressing issues of universal impact regardless of the source of poetic incentive: a wood-pile, a young beech or the "demands" of the new age of scientific and technological progress.

The Rhythm of the Walk/Poem: Human and Metrical Feet

The strongest evidence supporting the walk-poem comparison is, undoubtedly, the correspondence between human and metrical feet. The mood, the physical condition of the walker and the external conditions determine the speed and rhythm of each walk. As Ammons marks, whatever this rhythm is, "lumbering, clipped, wavering, tripping, mechanical, dance-like, awkward, staggering, [or] slow" it is "nonreproducible and nonlogical" because the motion occurs only "in the body of the walker or in the body of the words" (18). Observed from that perspective, the usage of the term "foot" in measuring the length of lines in poetry becomes much more meaningful, as well as the "beat" of stressed and unstressed syllables that determines the unique thythm of each poetic composition.

Ezra Pound's "A Few Don'ts by an Imagiste" (1913) marks an official shift in American poetry from the tradition of writing "in the sequence of the metronome" to composing in the "sequence of the musical phrase". Known for his distrust in nonmetrical poetry, Frost deviates from the tendency to swerve to free verse, continuing the tradition of the conventional iambic meter. Yet, even in the act of following the beaten track, Frost has left discernible personal footprints in American poetry. In "The Figue a Poem Makes", the New England poet's concern with the formal aspect of poetry finds reflection in the metaphor of the "straight crookedness of a good walking stick" that envisions the adherence to a specific metrical track as an indispensable aspect of worthy poetry. The reconciliation of the discordant words "straight" and "crooked" in the definition of the sole equipment of nature walks gives a clue about the nature of Frost's prosody.

The rigid pattern of weak and strong syllables in iambic compositions and the unbending sequence of the stressed and unstressed syllables of the trochaic meter can be successfully illustrated with the precise shape of a straight walking stick. Metric analysis of W.C. Bryant's "Thanatopsis" and E.A. Poe's "The Raven" will be of use to demonstrate this "straight" rhythmic pattern. Composed of a sequence of five iambic feet ("To **him**-who **in**-the **love**-of **na**-ture **holds**"[1]) the verses of "Thanatopsis" provides an exact illustration of iambic pentameter while the sequence of eight trochaic feet ("**Pro**fet-**said** I-**thing** of-**e**vil-**pro**fet-**still** if-**bird** or-**de**vil") turn Poe's work into a perfect example of trochaic octometer.

In contrast to his Romantic predecessors who apply a specific rhythmic pattern throughout the whole poetic composition, Frost deviates from the "straight" track of the familiar schemes and chooses the natural "crookedness" of fresh rhythmic tracks. "The Wood-Pile" offers different examples that illustrate how the rhythm of the poem reflects the hesitation of the walker, how the regularity of the standard iambic pentameter halts to mark the moments the speaker pauses to ruminate over what he sees. The following three lines illustrate the typical rhythm of the iambic pentameter:

> And **then**-there **was**-a **pile**-of **wood**-for **which**
> With**out**-so **much**-as **wish**-ing **him**-good **night**
> To **warm**-the **fro**-zen **swamp**-as **best**-it **could.** (18, 21, 39)

The opening lines signal the same rhythmic pattern yet the moment the speaker pauses finds reflection in the rhythm of the poem too with the additional half foot in the first line. Thus the last word "day" function as an extra step befor the "pause" reported in the next line:

> Out **walk**-ing **in**-the **fro**-zen **swamp**-one **gray day**
> I **paused**-and **said**-I **will**-turn **back**-from **here**.

---

[1] Bold characters are used to mark the stressed syllables and dashes are used to separate the feet in each line.

The spondaic emphasis achieved with the sequence of two stressed syllables ("gray day") virtually halts the rhythm of the line to mimic the rhythm of the walker's stride. It should be noted that the rest of the opening two lines follows the rhythmic pattern of the iambic pentameter only in technical terms. In the phrase "out walking", for example, normal pronunciation demands emphasis on the first syllable too ("**out walk**ing") to stress the direction of the movement ("out") to juxtapose it to the ensuing opposing direction ("in").

These examples show that the metric pattern of Frost's poetry is in tune with the themes he treats. Along with rhythm, this is valid for the organisation of his stanzas and the rhyme pattern of his works too. "A Passing Glimse", for example, reports how a person who normally observes reality as a walker, views "flowers from a passing car" or a "train". Ill-disposed to the speed of the vehicles, the speaker mentally reconstructs the scenes he sees from the familiar perspective of a walker. Composed in the form of six rhyming couplets, the poem recreates the act of walking. It seems that the speaker resists the speed of movement on four wheels clinging to the familiar sensation of the slow yet steady progress offerd by two legs. The pattern of the iambic pentameter that fits the rhythm of a regular walker, is disturbed though by the impact of the unaccustomed speed and the urge to restore the familiar pace of walking: "I **want** to get **out** of the **train** and go **back"** (3).

Frost's dexterity in using sound as sense is another stylistic hallmark that has received wide critical acclaim. "Stopping by Wooods on a Snowy Evening", for example, has been extensively praised for its power of turning the words into actants of the described winter scene. Lemaire observes the same skillfulness in the following lines of "A Leaf-Treader":

> I have been treading on leaves all day until I am autumn-
> tired.
> God knows all the color and form of leaves I have trodden
> on and mired.
> Perhaps I have put forth too much strength or been too
> fierce from fear.
> I have safely trodden underfoot the leaves of another year. (1-4)

Identifying the repetitive polyptotons "tread/treading/trodden", the critic discerns the "haunting musical transfer of the trampling sound of footsteps on the autumn leafy ground". Lemaire's critical lens also encompasses "the systematic run-on-lines which cut the staccato effect of the treading", the density of fricative and dental sounds ("treading, autumn, tired, trodden, put, too, strength, underfoot, form, forth, safely, leaves", and the "wind blowing-sounding ternary rhythm" of the alliterative expression "fierce from fear" (6).

The analysis of the rhythmic pattern and the sound effect of Frost's poetry justifies the walk-poem analogy and illustrates the aptness of the image of the "straight crookedness of a walking stick" for the characterization of the irregularity of the metric pattern of his works. Like the typical tone of indeterminacy that defines the walker in his works as a Romantic wanderer/wonderer with a modernist sensibility, the ruptures in the traditional rhythmic structure of his works signal deep awareness of the accelerated pace of the new modern world.

Conclusion

Robert Frost was largely dismissed by his contemporaries because of his outmoded insistence on traditional versification and his open hostility to free verse. The present study defines him as a figure who bridges his modernist insight with the poetic principles of his Romantic precursors by exploring the theme of walking in some of his poems. The investigation of the ways in which walking intersects with the act of thinking in these works shows that while some of Frost's poems are based on an explicit walk-poem or walker-poet analogy, others present the act of walking as a prelude to poetic creation or as a metaphor for the process of versification. The relationship between physical and metrical feet observed in the analysis of the rhythmic pattern of Frost's poems solidifies the walk-poem analogy and defines his speaker-poet as a walker who spans traditional form with modern awareness.

Bibliography

Ammons, A. R. "The Poem is a Walk." *Set in Motion: Essays, Interviews, and Dialogues,* edited by Zofia Burr, Michigan UP, 1996, pp. 12-20.

Bryant, William Cullen. "Lectures on Poetry." *Prose Writings of William Cullen Bryant*. vol. 1, edited by Parke Godwin, NY: Russel and Russel, 1964, pp.3-34.

Bryant, William Cullen. "On Trisyllabic Feet in Iambic Measure." *Prose Writings of William Cullen Bryant.* vol. 1, edited by Parke Godwin, NY: Russel and Russel, 1964, pp. 57-67.

Eliot, T.S. "The Lovesong of J. Alfred Pufrock."*The Norton Anthology of American Literature*, edited by Nina Baym, 4th ed., vol. 2, NY: Norton, 1994, pp. 1260-1263.

Emerson, Ralph W. "Apology." The American Tradition in Literature. Edited by Scully Bradley, 5th ed., vol. 1, NY: Random House, 1981, pp. 1415.

Emerson, Ralph W. "Thoreau." *The Norton Anthology of American Literature*, edited by Nina Baym, 4th ed., vol. 1, NY: Norton, 1994, pp. 1121-1133.

Crowley, J. Donald. "Hawthorne and Frost: The Making of a Poem." *Frost: Centennial Essays*. UP of Mississippi. 1973. maps-legacy.org/poets/a_f/frost/woodpile.htm.

Faggen, Robert. *Robert Frost and the Challenge of Darwin*. Ann Arbor: UP of Michigan, 1997. http://maps-legacy.org/poets/a_f/frost/woodpile.htm.

Frost, Robert. "Extaravgance." *Dartmouth Alumni Magazine*. March 1963, pp. 20-22.

Frost, Robert "The Figure a Poem Makes." *The Norton Anthology of American Literature*, edited by Nina Baym, 4th ed., vol. 2, NY: Norton, 1994, pp. 1114-1116.

Robert, Frost. *The Poetry of Robert Frost*, edited by Edward Connery Lathem, New York: Holt, Rinehart and Winston, 1975.

Lemaire, Candice. "The Constant Traveller: Staging Mobility in the Poetry of Robert Frost", *Miranda* [Online], 5/ 2011, URL: http://journals.openedition.org/miranda/2441; DOI: https://doi.org/10.4000/miranda.2441

Longfellow, Henry Wadsworth. "Defence of Poetry." *The North American Review*, vol. 34, Boston: Gray and Bowen, 1832, pp. 59-78.

Macgowain, Christopher. *Twenteeth-Century American Poetry.* Malden: Blackwell Publishing, 2005.

Meyer, Bruce. "Criticism on 'The Wood-Pile'". *Poetry for Students: Presenting Analysis, Context and Criticism on Commonly Studied Poetry*, edited by Mary K. Ruby, vol. 6, Detroit: Gale Group, 1999, pp. 257-260.

Pasquetti, Camila Alvares. "A Reading of Thoreau's 'Walking' as a Travel Narrative." MA Dissertation, Universidade Federal de Santa Catarina, 2005.

Pound, Ezra. "Hugh Selwyn Mauberley." *Heath Anthology of American Literature*, vol. 2, 2nd ed., edited by Paul Lauter, Lexington: D.C. Heath, 1994, pp.1209-1212.

Pritchard, William H. *Frost: A Literary Life Reconsidered.* Oxford: Oxford UP, 1984. maps-legacy.org/poets/a_f/frost/woodpile.htm.

Ruby, Mary K. (ed.) *Poetry for Students: Presenting Analysis, Context and Criticism on Commonly Studied Poetry.* vol. 6, Detroit: Gale Group, 1999.

Starr, G. Gabrielle. "Motion in Stevens and Frost." *Wallace Stevens Journal*, vol. 41, no. 1, Spring 2017, pp. 90-92.

Thoreau, Henry David. From *Walden. United States in Literature*, edited by James E. Miller, Glenview: Scott, Foresman and Company, 1979, pp. 232-239.

Thoreau "Walking". *Heath Anthology of American Literature*, vol. 1, 2nd ed., edited by Paul Lauter, Lexington: D.C. Heath, 1994, pp. 2079-2100.

Whitman, Walt. "Song of Myself." *Heath Anthology of American Literature*, vol. 1, 2nd ed., edited by Paul Lauter, Lexington: D.C. Heath, 1994, pp. 2758-2808.

Short Bio of Prof. Dr. Hasine Şen KARADENİZ

Prof. Dr. Hasine Şen Karadeniz earned her MA and PhD from Istanbul University, the Department of American Culture and Literature. Currently she teaches graduate and postgraduate courses on American Literature at the same institution. She is the author of *The Borderland as a Site of Resistance to Boundaries: Discussion of Identity in the Chicano/a Novel* (2011), *The Power of Silence: Exploration of Muteness in Jerzy Kosinski's The Painted Bird and Ken Kesey's One Flew Over the Cuckoo's Nest* (2018) and articles on American poetry, migration, the Balkans and Balkan literature.

Traveling Between the Lines in T.S. Eliot's "The Love Song of Alfred Prufrock"

Prof. Dr. Meryem AYAN and Res. Assist. Dr. Özlem YILMAZ

Abstract

The origins of travel writing can be grounded in the literary texts of ancient times. travel writing as a specific and indigenous genre is a relatively recent focus of interest among literary critics, the popularity of which increases day by day. Travel writing is all about experiences one has during a journey, and writing is one of the outlets of the traveler's experiences and her/his views during the travel. Namely, travel writing presents the subjective observations of a traveler who is moving between the material and imaginary realms. Eliot's poem "The Love Song of J. Alfred Prufrock" is frequently studied in terms of the modernist characteristics it involves as well as of its embodiment of almost "every important innovation in the English verse" of the early twentieth century (Sultan 89). However, the fact that no study steps ahead in the literature which scrutinizes the poem in the framework of the travel writing genre opens the way for further investigation. Hence, the aim of this study is to analyze the poem by focusing on the mental journey that J. Alfred Prufrock invites the reader to witness while he travels between the lines so as to demonstrate that the poem can be considered an unusual but successful example of travel writing. Namely, Eliot's poem, "The Love Song of J. Alfred Prufrock" presents a literary journey between the lines drawing a portrait of the mental journey of a man whose mental travel can be considered an example of travel writing.

Keywords: Travel Writing, T.S. Eliot, "The Love Song of Alfred Prufrock", Mental journey, and Travelogue

Introduction: Travel Writing

The origins of travel writing can be grounded in the literary texts of ancient times, travel writing as a specific and indigenous genre is a relatively recent focus of interest among literary critics, the popularity of which increases day by day. Travel writing is all about experiences one has during a journey, and writing is one of the outlets of the traveler's experiences and her/his views during the travel. Namely, travel writing presents the subjective observations of a traveler who is moving between the material and imaginary realms.

In the broadest sense, travel writing can be defined as all kinds of texts that depict a physical journey, including accounts openly acknowledging their entirely fictitious nature. Travel writing can be defined as a "frictional literature" that "oscillates between fictional and factual writing" (Ette 31) because it is a hybrid genre that borders on, as well as incorporates, elements of various other text types such as novels, autobiographies, reports, legends, diaries, letters, tracts, or essays, and may, therefore, be difficult to distinguish from them" (Ette 25–26). On the other hand, from a narrow perspective, travel writing can be limited to denote only narratives of actual travels penned with a subjective, "literary purpose" and the intention of public dissemination (Blanton 4–5).

Generally, travel writing is a key source of information about the outside world. It has influenced the explorations, and development of fields such as science, history, literature etc. Travel writing is all documented in the form of literary texts called travel narratives. There has always been an interconnected link between travel and literature, since, as Mewshaw states, travel has always been "the basic underpinning or subtext of a lot of literature which we would not normally associate with travel" (4). A "transportation revolution" occurred between 1815 and 1860, in George Roger Taylor's words, who used the term for the first time to "describe the effect that technological and financial improvements had on the commercial and industrial development of the United States between 1815 and 1860" (Mackintosh 62). Although Taylor's definition stems from the developments which were observed during "the Industrial Revolution in the United States, the same transformation was more severely experienced in Britain too, and probably earlier than in the United States since Britain was the first nation to move from an agricultural nation to an industrial one" (Mackintosh 62). In both Britain and America, as well as in other European countries, at the "core of [this] revolutionary change" lied "the cheapening and facilitating of the movement of goods and persons" (ibid 62). As a result of the decrease which occurred in the financial costs of travel, it became something affordable for many people, as well as an easier one, which was a great transformation in the history of travel. This transformation which was inaugurated with the effect of the acceleration of industrialization at the beginning of the nineteenth century gained more speed as the century progressed since it was carried forward by turnpikes in the 1810s and 1820s and by canals in the 1820s and 1830s" (Mackintosh 62). As a result of the appearance and swift expansion of steamboats and railroads, travel became "significantly faster, much more reliable, and considerably more economical in the 1840s" (62). Thus, during the 18th century, travel writing was known as the Book of Travels. Most travel books contained factual journeys. In the late 19th century, many started exploring regions other than continental Europe and indulged in travel documentation to serve as a reference to future explorers. Thus, travel writing evolved as an important genre in the field of literature presenting accounts of the narrator's both physical and mental journey. Richardson wrote about the difficulties of traveling and stated that in that time interval traveling was executed "in perpetual anxiety" (Mackintosh 61). He also expressed that most of the travelers had difficulties in finding their way, they "worried constantly about finding food, lodging, and about losing [their] horses", as well as their "sanity", thus, stating that [their] journey was "tedious beyond description" (Mackintosh 61). Hence, the kind of difficulties travelers were bound to face and the adventures they came across in their journeys constituted a fertile ground for writers during the eighteenth and nineteenth centuries. However, the nineteenth century witnessed a gradual change in the traveling concept, which naturally found its reflections in the literary arena too.

Naturally, all these developments led to considerable changes in the understanding of the concept of travel too, since it became something less individual and private, but more public and commercial. While at the beginning of the nineteenth-century travelers "thought of their travel as something that they produced themselves, out of the raw materials of geographical knowledge, means of transportation, and provisions for the road", as the century progressed towards the twentieth, it became unnecessary to have the sufficiency or expertise to know "where to go, how best to get there, and what the current conditions along [the] route were" (Mackintosh 63). This "changing experience of travel" still appealed more to the middle and upper classes rather than to the working class, and they "slowly became passengers" rather than travelers, which meant that they were now the "consumers of travel rather than producers of" it (66). As people "began to think about travel as a commodity" and concentrated on its "affordability, reliability, and convenience" (ibid 66), unfortunately, traveling faced the loss of romantic pleasure, which was one of its indispensable elements of it. As early as 1840, for instance, Louis Tasistro "used the language of romanticism to express skepticism about commodified travel when he wondered how much [was] lost of nature's grandeur and loveliness to him who catche[d] but a passing view of either, as he hurrie[d] along in a stagecoach" (87).

Expectedly there were some developments that triggered the critical turning point in the history of travel, which also demonstrated itself in literature not only in the specific form of travel writing but also in other genres such as poetry and novel, which fed from the romantic concept of travel considerably. At the beginning of the twentieth century "with the development of the motor car and the cargo truck", along with the expansion of mass transportation "organic mode of individual travel" lost its place completely (Rosler 111). As travel became more and more commodified towards the end of the century, travelers who had a more romantic understanding of travel began to lose their interest in the act of traveling. As Bryce states, they began to think that they would rather "occupy themselves by thinking about travelling" (110). This loss of interest showed itself in the representation of travel stories in literature too, which was a kind of death blow to the literary imagination since writers "need[ed] travel, its freedom, its stimulation, and exposure to new and innovative points of view in the same way they need[ed] air, editors, and a reading audience" (Mewshaw 3). Therefore, as Paul Fussell claimed, there was an unavoidable "loss of amplitude", as well as "a decay of imagination and intellectual possibility corresponding to the literal loss of physical freedom" (qtd in Mewshaw 3). Hence, travel's romantic glow was lost not only for writers and poets but also for many people with romantic spirits.

When the twentieth century began, "according to some critics and cavillers, travel no longer exist[ed]. It [was] all replaced by the plague of tourism" (Mewshaw 2), and the concept of the "authentic traveller" had already "left its place to mechanized tourists" (2), thus, leaving no place for romantic imagination. It was during this time that T.S. Eliot wrote "The Love Song of J. Alfred Prufrock". As Peterson states, T. S. Eliot, followed the trail of modernism in his poetry (20). He "generally expose[d] humanity's crippling insecurity" and "connect[ed) it interpersonally in meaningful ways" (20), which can also be related to his preference for documenting a mental journey in the poem through an insecure male narrator. As a result of the decadent ideas which spread in fin de siècle and because of the early modernist emphasis on individualism that prevailed in British society and literature at the beginning of the twentieth century, a rising interest occurred in the human psyche along with the development of the science of psychiatry.

With the decadent and modernist influences, many people preferred to turn inside and investigate their own selves, simultaneously feeling a necessity to escape the hypocrisy of society. For these people, public transportation which clearly lacked any privacy was not a suitable means of traveling since all the romantic pleasure embodied in the individual traveling concept was lost. The disappearance of the romantic aspect of traveling resulted in the loss of that special feeling that "Wallace Stevens called the pleasures of merely circulating" (Mewshaw 2). However, travel meant something larger than that romantic pleasure.

As Freud suggested, "a great part of the pleasure" was related to the "fulfillment of [...] early wishes to escape" (qtd in Mewshaw 2). Moving from Freud's emphasis on traveling as a way of the escapement, it can be concluded that travel can be seen as a liminal space that functions as a gateway between any disturbing context surrounding the individual and the desired place. Therefore, "mental traveling" can be interpreted to be signifying another kind of escape; an escape from material reality towards an imaginary realm, which either forecasts future episodes or flashbacks to previous memories. Albeit this might seem antithetical, the possibility of the opening of this double-acting door in the human brain is scientifically approved by various scholars working in different areas of research.

Considering that any kind of writing which involves an account of the journey in it "even if the journey is entirely inward" can be classified as an example of travel writing (Mewshaw 9), T.S. Eliot's poem "The Love Song of J. Alfred Prufrock" can certainly be classified under this category too, which constitutes the focal point of this study.

Mental Travel in Eliot's "The Love Song of Alfred Prufrock"

Eliot's poem "The Love Song of J. Alfred Prufrock" is frequently studied in terms of the modernist characteristics it involves as well as of its embodiment of almost "every important innovation in the English verse" of the early twentieth century (Sultan 89). However, the fact that no study steps ahead in the litterateur which scrutinizes the poem in the framework of the travel writing genre opens the way for further investigation. Hence, the aim of this study is to analyze the poem by focusing on the mental journey that J. Alfred Prufrock invites the reader to witness while he travels between the lines so as to demonstrate that the poem can be considered an unusual but successful example of travel writing. Namely, Eliot's poem, "The Love Song of J. Alfred Prufrock" presents a literary journey between the lines drawing a portrait of the mental journey of a man whose mental travel can be considered an example of travel writing.

Actually, the title "The Love Song of J. Alfred Prufrock" is ironic because it associates a romantic poem, but Prufrock never talks about his feelings of love or his love toward his beloved one throughout the poem but about his hesitations, traumas, and loneliness. Thus, the poem rather than presenting romantic feelings narrates the pathetic feelings of an isolated and indecisive man. In other words, Eliot portrays the complex journey of a middle-aged named Prufrock who cannot progress in life and does not have the courage to approach women, due to his timidity and lack of self-confidence. The poetic voice, Prufrock both on two-sided travel one is an outward physical journey toward old age, and the other one is an inward mental journey enabling him to travel back and forth in an imaginary world.

Actually, the theory of mind originates from the idea that it is possible for humankind to "wander" back and forth through time mentally, into both "imaginary worlds" and "minds of others" since the human brain has "evolved" to execute this kind of mobility in time (Corballis 888). Although the theory envisions that this movement occurs not only in time but also in "what others think or believe", the key concept of "mental travel" mainly refers to a kind of journey that takes place in the mental sphere and enables not only a recollection of the past memories but also the imagination of future ones (870), which can be observed in Eliot's poem, too. The concept of "mental travel" was first introduced by Endel Tulving in 1972, which he coined while "investigating the difference between episodic and semantic memories" (874). This difference was brought to attention during "the investigation of a neurologic case, the case of a patient named Clive Wearing" (Suddendorf et al 1317). The analysis of this patient with amnesia "illustrated the distinction between semantic memory, which is the memory for enduring facts about the world, and episodic memory, which is a personal record of the past" (Tulving qtd. in Suddendorf et al 1317). It was during this analysis that the possibility of mental travel was discovered, and it was observed that this took place with the help of episodic memory. Episodic memory was found to be granting humankind not only "the ability to bring to mind past events" but also "imagining future ones", which made it possible to "mentally escape the present and wander into past and future and into the minds of others". (Corballis 870). Cutting our connection with the present tense and current environment, "the default mode" which takes place in "the brain with the functioning of episodic memory was found to be enabling us to escape to another imaginary world" (870), which as readers we can witness in Prufrock's mental journey while we travel with him between the lines.

The poem has a "canonical status" in English literature, in 1959 it was referred to the "the best-known English poem since the Rubaiyat" and is still assumed to be one of the best poems written in the English language (Sultan 77). It is known that Eliot "began drafting parts of The Love Song of J. Alfred Prufrock in 1909 and it took 6 years for him to publish it" (Peterson 23). In 1915, Eliot submitted it to the reader's discretion and presented them with a dramatic monologue. The poem is frequently discussed regarding split-identity discussions, and it is claimed by many critics that the narrator is talking to his divided self. One of these critics, for instance, states that "Prufrock speaks not to the reader but to the two elements of himself, the surface objective-passive milquetoast who does not dare to eat a peach and the inward subjective-active-macho-ego who would dare if he could get out" (Smith 705). This implies that the journey reader comes across in the poem takes place in the narrator's psyche, in which the starting point is one element of the narrator's personality while the arrival point is another.

The epigraph of the poem is a six-line quotation from Canto 27 of the Italian poet's *Inferno*, which can be translated into English briefly as:

> If I thought my reply was given to anyone who might return to the world, this flame would stand forever still; but since never from this deep place has anyone returned alive, if what I hear is true, without the fear of infamy I answer thee" ("Guida da Montefeltro").

The epigraph presents the reader with the subject of death, with an implication that the narrator is dreaming of a journey that would take him to the end of his life. Although the epigraph is ambiguous about whether this death that the narrator is imagining has already taken place in the past or if he is forecasting a future scene, the desired moment in which he comes back from death; overall scrutiny of the poem reveals that the narrator is in expectation of death, rather than memorizing the death of a loved one. Despite the ambiguity of these lines, it is clear that he is taking a mental journey in his mind and moving across time – either backward to memory or forward to an imagined moment, which is in accordance with Corballis's definition of mental traveling in which he claims that it is possible to achieve mobility and "wander back and forth through time mentally" (870). This mental journey which is presented to the reader as early as in the epigraph expands all over the poem which is quite apparent in the first stanza:

Let us go then, you and I,
When the evening is spread out against the sky
Like a patient etherized upon a table;
Let us go, through certain half-deserted streets,
The muttering retreats
Of restless nights in one-night cheap hotels
And sawdust restaurants with oyster-shells:
Streets that follow like a tedious argument
Of insidious intent
To lead you to an overwhelming question ...
Oh, do not ask, "What is it?"
Let us go and make our visit

The mental journey that the reader goes through is quite apparent in these lines since he clearly longs for achieving mobility in time so as to leap forward to an evening hour. The poem opens with an invitation "Let us go then, you and I". This can be interpreted as the travelogue of Prufrock talking both to himself and the reader. The "you" is the passionate self who insists on going to make the visit. The "I" is the one who consents and invites "you" to join him on this mental journey. If in the epigraph we had Guido's answer to Dante, somebody who, he believed, would never return to the world to report Guido's words, now in the poem, we have the words of the condemned "I" who, like Guido, speak freely only because he is sure that the "you" will not tell anybody about him. Onand the other hand, Prufrock is trying to commute with the reader as a confidant or confidante to share his secrets regarding his inner world. Namely, Prufrock's travelogue is inviting the reader to join him on a mental journey in which he would confess his secrets, envies, passions, and regrets within the lines of the poem that would enable him to move back and forth between the factual and fictional borders of the words.

Imagining that he is experiencing an evening that spreads out against the sky, the narrator named Prufrock is nevertheless aware of the fact, that he is just mentally traveling to that time interval and temporarily moving away from reality. The third line of the poem "like a patient etherized upon a table" is significant in terms of its demonstration of the mental characteristic of the narrator's journey since it indicates a lot about the narrator's flight from the real world, in accordance with Corballis's explanation of the "default mode" (870) which takes place in the human brain during mental traveling and cuts the connection with the present tense and current environment. Having cut his connection with the real world, the narrator is like a patient who is etherized in the operating room. Although his body is physically present in the real world, his mind is somewhere else. Regarding the presence of a mental journey in this stanza of the poem, Peterson affirmatively states that in its "first twelve lines", the poem "pose[s]the problem of our narrator who must reluctantly take a mental journey to resolve his famously unspecified (oh do not ask, What is it?) question and "prepares himself for a deep psychological journey" (23). Eliot does not provide names for his characters except Prufrock who reflects the hardships people face when focusing on their own dreams and individualism during their journey through life.

Prufrock continues his journey. He sees women talking about Michelangelo, but the women exactly do not know who Michelangelo. In fact, Prufrock imagines some women walking around in the room and talking about Michelangelo and when is trapped in hesitation, these women's imaginaries in his head talk about Michelangelo, who is a courageous, young, and perfect male feature with great energy. Unconsciously, he begins to compare himself with the perfect image of Michelangelo, but then realizes that there is a great distance between himself and Michelangelo. Thus, the ideal image inside his head makes him look down upon his usual behaviors and to examine himself in a disdainful manner of self-denial and uneasy. Prufrock repeats these lines later again indicating his mental journey:

In the room the women come and go
Talking of Michelangelo.

The narrator, Prufrock's mental turbidity continues to be observed in the following lines too, in which the fog symbolizes "Prufrock's mental state, which clearly "lacks any resolution" (Peterson 23) and is in a pessimistic mood:

The yellow fog that rubs its back upon the window panes,
The yellow smoke that rubs its muzzle on the window panes,
Licked its tongue into the corners of the evening,
Lingered upon the pools that stand in drains,
Let fall upon its back the soot that falls from chimneys,
Slipped by the terrace, made a sudden leap,
And seeing that it was a soft October night,
Curled once about the house and fell asleep.

Towards the end of the first stanza, Prufrock makes "a sudden leap" and moves backward in time to a memory that took place on an October night, which, again, demonstrates his ability to move across time to realize a restoration of memories. Typical of the back-and-forth movements mentioned in the theory of mind, right after this stanza he moves from the past to the future, skipping the present tense and imagining future times where he will meet new faces as the following lines demonstrate:

> And indeed there will be time
> For the yellow smoke that slides along the street,
> Rubbing its back upon the window-panes;
> There will be time, there will be time
> To prepare a face to meet the faces that you meet.
> There will be time to murder and create,
> And time for all the works and days of hands
> That lift and drop a question on your plate;
> Time for you and time for me,
> And time yet for a hundred indecisions,
> And for a hundred visions and revisions,
> Before taking of a toast and tea.

Prufrock's expression "there will be time" is ironic because he longs for his death, which he dreams of as his last journey. Therefore, he dreams of those future days in which he is old and close to his divine ending. Prufrock's repetition of "there will be time" reflects his dream, desire, and the imaginative world but in the physical world there is fragmentation and frustration, therefore in the real world, there will be no time for anything because no matter how much time there is, no matter how he thinks about it, there is going to no right time to achieve his goals. In other words, Prufrock tries to be self-satisfied by the repetitive usage of "There will be time, there will be time" but in terms of action, he postpones doing things all the time because he is a "typical passive procrastinator" (Qiao & Miao 269) postponing his tasks until the last minute with feelings of fear, depression, and hesitation.

Prufrock repeats the lines "In the room, the women come and go/Talking of Michelangelo" indicating that time and life is repetitive and dull. Prufrock observes the hypocrisy within society and his relations with women. In fact, Prufrock is a character full of conflicts and he is envying love but fears of the idea of falling in love, therefore, he is anxious, hesitant inaction, and indecisive. He cannot show his love to the lady whom he loves, and his cowardice makes him constantly avoid having a true love relation with a woman. At the same time, it fails him in meeting the satisfaction of his primal instinct. Prufrock seems to have frustrated feelings and thoughts about women therefore he presents women as passengers coming and going in his life. Prufrock is mocking the way people and the woman who he met are talking about things they have no relevant knowledge on but have just heard or learned during their insincere conversations. Namely, Prufrock is also very critical of people's and women's hypocrisy. Thus, he believes that the women who talk about Michelangelo do not know anything about either the artist or his paintings; however, to him, they just undertake such a task as it was fashionable to speak about artistic works among people. Prufrock is confused about himself in every situation because he knows other people very well. He is knowledgeable, but others are not knowledgeable like him. Thus, it creates a gap between them, and it is not possible for Prufrock to unite with them or talk with them on a physical journey.

As the following lines demonstrate, the poem presents the concept of aging as an example of moving forward in time in the framework of a mental journey:

> And indeed, there will be time
> To wonder, "Do I dare?" and, "Do I dare?"
> Time to turn back and descend the stair,
> With a bald spot in the middle of my hair —
> (They will say: "How his hair is growing thin!")
> My morning coat, my collar mounting firmly to the chin,
> My necktie rich and modest, but asserted by a simple pin —
> (They will say: "But how his arms and legs are thin!")

Prufrock's overwhelming emotions come to a full appearance in this stanza. He insists that 'there will be a time' when he will dare to express his feelings and passions, but he is getting old and there is no strength left to move further so he dreams about those days when he is close to death. Schneider states that "certainly trivialities abound proper neckties, artistic small talk, and the rest. That is the kind of society in which Prufrock moves, and, obviously, there is boredom in the empty fullness of its life" (1104). Indeed, Prufrock is in conflict with himself which shows he is aware of the hypocrisy of the society he lives in, and he feels insecure about his own appearance because he is becoming less attractive and more indecisive as time passes, and as he grows old. The parenthesis in the above quotation reflects Prufrock's anxiety about public opinion because he feels inferior and is worried about how his appearance will be evaluated by others.

In the following stanzas, Prufrock makes a calculation of life indicating he had experienced everything and was familiar with life, but he has wasted his life attending trivial tea parties. He claims: “I have measured out my life with coffee spoons”.

> For I have known them all already, known them all:
> Have known the evenings, mornings, afternoons,
> I have measured out my life with coffee spoons;
> I know the voices dying with a dying fall
> Beneath the music from a farther room.
> So how should I presume?

The objective correlative expression of life: “I have measured out my life with coffee spoons” indicates that Prufrock has led a limited and unsatisfying life because he has done everything already. He is trying to convince us that he’s a wise man with lots of experience therefore, he does not need to do anything, because measured his whole life. He knows "the voices dying with a dying fall" but he could not do anything for them except to sit and look because he has no courage and strength.

Prufrock is talking about the things he knows but everything is becoming unknown because he does not have the courage to act and prevent the phoniness in the world.

> And I have known the eyes already, known them all—
> The eyes that fix you in a formulated phrase,
> And when I am formulated, sprawling on a pin,
> When I am pinned and wriggling on the wall,
> Then how should I begin
> To spit out all the butt-ends of my days and ways?
> And how should I presume?

Prufrock says he knows the eyes, that gaze at him and stuck him to the wall. Namely, he is referring to the hypocritical people who formulated him. They fix him to the wall, and he is sprawling on a pin because they are the dominating people in this society. He feels stuck and helpless and unable to do anything. He questions his situation but does not know how to adjust to everything again because he is getting old and does not have the power to struggle with the hypocritical people shaping his life.

He continues remembering his past days and says that he knows the women's arms, which are braceleted and white and bare in the following stanza:

> And I have known the arms already, known them all—
> Arms that are braceleted and white and bare
> (But in the lamplight, downed with light brown hair!)
> Is it perfume from a dress
> That makes me so digress?
> Arms that lie along a table or wrap about a shawl.
> And should I then presume?
> And how should I begin?

Prufrock, in the framework of a mental journey, is addressing the woman he knows or remembers that she exists, he knows who she is, and he thinks of her in terms of arms, eyes, and bracelets, but he cannot approach her. Remembering only the arm and the bracelets Oedipus Complex that occurs during a child's psychological development. Namely, the Oedipus Complex is a problem that occurs in a boy during the phallic stage in which the Oedipus complex, or, conflict, arises because the boy develops unconscious sexual desires for his mother and feels envy and jealousy towards the father. The unconscious feelings are repressed because of the fear of displeasure or punishment by the parents of the same sex. Thus, the poetic persona Prufrock has mental problems supposing to his parental relations and especially his mother. Furthermore, Prufrock by asking "Is it perfume from a dress / That makes me so digress? is questioning the factual and fictional relations that he had or made up in his psychic world. In fact, Prufrock is self-aware enough to know that his attempt to remember the past and keep back will not make him happy.. He is in agony because of his crippling shyness and insecurity, he is scared to talk to the women he sees. He does not think the women will be interested in him and will not be able to articulate his feelings well enough because he cannot express his true feelings. Thus, he has hesitations, and rather than talking with the women, he talks with himself which indicates that he is alone and has no one to trust and speak to but only himself that becomes a monologue physically but a dialogue mentally because he is talking with and to himself in loneliness.

Prufrock is aware of his own loneliness and reduces himself to an animal, living alone, sheltered at the bottom of the dark ocean as seen in the following stanza:

> Shall I say, I have gone at dusk through narrow streets
> And watched the smoke that rises from the pipes
> Of lonely men in shirt-sleeves, leaning out of windows? ...
> I should have been a pair of ragged claws
> Scuttling across the floors of silent seas.

Prufrock's desire to be an inanimate object like "a pair of ragged claws" that shows he wants to escape from the hypocrisy and loneliness that is surrounding him. Namely, he wants to escape the epiphany world and be secure as an animal at the bottom of the silent sea.

Prufrock's in following stanza shows that he knows very well how to speak in his own mind to himself but he cannot communicate with others around him:

> And the afternoon, the evening, sleeps so peacefully!
> Smoothed by long fingers,
> Asleep ... tired ... or it malingers,
> Stretched on the floor, here beside you and me.
> Should I, after tea and cakes and ices,
> Have the strength to force the moment to its crisis?
> But though I have wept and fasted, wept and prayed,
> Though I have seen my head (grown slightly bald) brought in upon a platter,
> I am no prophet — and here's no great matter.
> I have seen the moment of my greatness flicker,
> And I have seen the eternal Footman hold my coat, and snicker,
> And in short, I was afraid.

The problem of Prufrock is the traumas that avoid him from voicing his true feelings and thoughts. He expresses that he is not a prophet but has experienced bad things that have scared him as the eternal Footman holding his coat, referring to timeless death fear. In the following stanza, he turns back and evaluates his life:

And would it have been worth it, after all,
After the cups, the marmalade, the tea,
Among the porcelain, among some talk of you and me,
Would it have been worthwhile,
To have bitten off the matter with a smile,
To have squeezed the universe into a ball
To roll it towards some overwhelming question,
To say: "I am Lazarus, come from the dead,
Come back to tell you all, I shall tell you all"—
If one, settling a pillow by her head
Should say: "That is not what I meant at all.
That is not it, at all."

In the above stanza, Prufrock utters violent words: 'to have bitten off the matter with a smile / to have squeezed the universe into a ball.' Here, Prufrock fantasizes that he has had a change of heart and gone to speak to the woman at the center of the poem, picturing himself as Lazarus "come back from the dead, " which shows Prufrock's academic and biblical background. Prufrock thinks while drinking tea or he will use all his strength to transform the world into a ball by pressure and roll it toward some overwhelming question. Or he will die like Lazarus and come back again, and he will tell the whole world what the pain after death is. He is overcoming his crippling shyness.

And would it have been worth it, after all,
Would it have been worthwhile,
After the sunsets and the dooryards and the sprinkled streets,
After the novels, after the teacups, after the skirts that trail along the floor—
And this, and so much more? —
It is impossible to say just what I mean!
But as if a magic lantern threw the nerves in patterns on a screen:
Would it have been worth while
If one, settling a pillow or throwing off a shawl,
And turning toward the window, should say:
That is not it at all,
That is not what I meant, at all.

Prufrock almost seems to have raised his spirits enough to attempt to speak to the women at the center of the poem in the above stanza but fails to start the conversation by stating "That is not what I meant at all."

No! I am not Prince Hamlet, nor was meant to be;
Am an attendant lord, one that will do
To swell a progress, start a scene or two,
Advise the prince, no doubt, an easy tool,
Deferential, glad to be of use,
Politic, cautious, and meticulous;
Full of high sentence, but a bit obtuse;
At times, indeed, almost ridiculous—
Almost, at times, the Fool.

Prufrock, in this stanza once again reduces himself again to the part of the fool, shrinking himself down from the heroic stature that he has built up in the previous two stanzas. He says, comparing himself with Prince Hamlet. "No! I am not Prince Hamlet, nor was meant to be". Although Hamlet is hesitant in the process of revenge, he sticks to his own determination and enthusiasm while fighting all the difficulties and obstacles. Yet, Prufrock is not Hamlet, he is not perfect, and leads a vacuous life, which in turn aggravates his self-doubt, self-abasement, and procrastination.

Prufrock's a fraction of his former self because it is getting harder for him to cope with life because he is getting older, and his inner struggles and hesitations are increasing. As Hakac asserts a state of "inertia" prevails in the poem (52).

I grow old ... I grow old ...
I shall wear the bottoms of my trousers rolled.
Shall I part my hair behind? Do I dare to eat a peach?
I shall wear white flannel trousers and walk upon the beach.
I have heard the mermaids singing, each to each.
I do not think that they will sing to me.
I have seen them riding seaward on the waves
Combing the white hair of the waves blown back
When the wind blows the water white and black.
We have lingered in the chambers of the sea
By sea-girls wreathed with seaweed red and brown
Till human voices wake us, and we drown.

In the last part of the poem, there is a great change: from a tone of self-mockery. In fact, Prufrock realizes that time is passing and that he is growing old. However, like other men going through a middle-age crisis, he considers changing his hairstyle and clothes. Like Odysseus in the Odyssey, he has heard the song of the sirens. However, they are not singing to him. Prufrock in the end tries to escape from the real world where he was defeated, and he dreams of mermaids. Yet he cannot avoid reality and physically drowns in them, but mentally travels in the imagination.

Conclusion: Travelogue between the Lines

Eliot's poem is a song of desire and failure and a travel story of what is taking place inside the travelogue of a man called Prufrock, Thus, as a dramatic monologue, the poem is presenting the mental journey of a traveler who for years has gained experience and turned into a mature person whose memories are reports of his life travel. Since the poem embodies physical aging along with the mental memorization of the old traveler whose travelogue indicates that he has no strength left to travel further in life. He is aware of his weakness and disabilities: "I have seen the moment of my greatness flicker, / and I have seen the eternal Footman hold my coat, and snicker" (lines 84-85), therefore Prufrock is expecting death to arrive and take him on his last eternal journey because is an unhappy frustrated man. Namely, J. Alfred Prufrock is conditioned by the fashionable society that made him tired due to the superficial and miserable events in his life. Besides, he is isolated in the world he both knows well and feels isolated. He has a range of more or less obscure feelings that he cannot communicate due to his inhibitions and timidity, thus he talks to himself, and he suffers. In fact, Prufrock is a literary figure who has been a voice representing the lack of communication and isolation of modern city life.

Consequently, Prufrock lives in a self-made fictional world, therefore factual world seems to be far away from him. In the end, like an invisible man, he continues to travel mentally alone in his own mental world. Thus, the poem can be seen as a travelogue of Prufrock and a travel guide of a mental journey that is presenting the travel story of a man who is mentally traveling back and forth between the lines of a fictional work.

Bibliography

Blanton, Casey. *Travel Writing: The Self and the World*. New York: Routledge. 2002.

Bryce, Viscount. "The Mental Training of a Traveller". *The Geographical Journal*. Vol. 45. 2, pp. 110-122.

Corballis, Michael C. "The Wandering Mind: Mental Time Travel, Theory of Mind and Language". *Analise Social*. 2012, Vol 47. 205, pp.870-893.

Eliot, T.S. *Let Us Go Than You and I: Selected Poems*. Faber & Faber, 2009 "Guida da Montefeltro: Circle 8, Inferno 27". https://danteworlds.laits.utexas.edu/textpopup/inf2701.html. Access 9 September 2022.

Ette, Ottmar. Literature on the Move. Trans. Katharina Vester. Amsterdam: Rodopi. 2003

Hakac, John. "The Yellow Fog of Prufrock". *The Bulletin of the Rocky Mountain Modern Language Association*. June 1972, Vol. 26. 2, pp.52-54.

Locke, Frederick W. "T.S. Eliot's Prufrock". *MLN*. January 1963, Vol. 78.1. pp. 51-59.

Mackintosh, Will. "Ticketed Through: The Commodification of Travel in the Nineteenth Century: *Journal of the Early Republic*. Spring 2012, Vol. 32. 1.pp 61-89.

Mewshaw, Michael. "Travel, Travel Writing, and the Literature of Travel". *South Central Review*. Summer 2005, Vol. 22, 2, pp. 2-10.

Peterson, Rai. "The Women Come and Go Sonnet Cycles in T.S. Eliot and E.E. Cummings". *Spring*. October 2011, No. 18, pp.20-34.

Qiad, Dan-Qiu, & Li-Yao Miao, "Procrastination: A Psychological Study on the Love Song of J. Alfred Prufrock" Advances in Social Science, Education and Humanities Research, volume 28 (14th International Conference on Social Science and Contemporary Humanity Development (SSCHD 2018) Atlantis Press 2019, pp. 269-273

Rosler, Martha. "Travel Stories". *Grey Room*. Summer 2002, 8, pp.108-137.

Schneider, Elizabeth. "Prufrock and After: The Theme of Change". *PMLA*. October 1972, Vol. 87. 5, pp.1103-1118.

Smith, Wendell H. "A Comment on Prufrock's Grammar". *College English*. February 1979. Vol. 40.6. pp. 705-706.

Suddendorf, Thomas, Donna Rose Addis &Michael C. Corballis. "Mental Time Travel and the Shaping of the Human Mind". *Philosophical Transactions: Biological Sciences*. May 12, 2009, Vol. 364. 1521, pp.1317-1324.

Sultan, Stanley. "Tradition and the Individual Talent in Prufrock". *Journal of Modern Literature*. March 1985, 12.1, pp. 77-90.

Short Bio of Prof. Dr. Meryem AYAN

Prof. Dr. Meryem AYAN graduated from Ege University, English Literature and Language Department, in 1992, and received her MA from the same department in 1997. She received her PhD from Dokuz Eylül University, American Culture and Literature Department, with her thesis entitled, "The Ghosts of the Past in ethnic Female Literature", in 2002. For seventeen years she worked at Pamukkale University. At present, she is working as a Professor Dr. at Celal Bayar University, English Language and Literature Department, Manisa. Her main interests are female identities, place and narration in ethnic women's novels, feminism, cultural studies, and gender studies.

Short Bio of Res. Assist. Özlem YILMAZ

Res. Assit. Dr. Özlem YILMAZ graduated from Manisa Celal Bayar University, English Literature and Language Department and received her MA from the same department. She received her PhD from İzmir Democracy University, in 2021. At present, she is working as a Res. Assist. Dr. at Celal Bayar University, English Language and Literature Department, Manisa. Her main interests are comparative literature, masculine and gender studies,

The Sense of Dissatisfaction as a source for Epiphany in Jack Kerouac's *On the Road*

Assoc. Prof. Dr. Zennure KÖSEMAN

Abstract

This article highlights that lack of satisfaction is a means of traveling as reflected in Jack Kerouac's *On the Road.* As a great masterpiece of the Beat Generation in the post war era of the 1950s, Kerouac emphasizes the state of loneliness and alienation deriving from individuals' state of dissatisfaction. As a literary movement, Beat Generation implies the weariness of individuals from their conventional worlds so that they depict their purposelessness in their modern world while caring for freedom in nature. Leading a free life drives them to visit new places to find themselves better through having new friendships. Revolting at their loneliness and alienation, they revive themselves through traveling. To illustrate, Sal Paradise becomes a new person while traveling with his penniless friends. When they admire new visiting areas, they have satisfaction with themselves. Through their frantic trips in United States, penniless young individuals become content with the time, beauty, jazz and drugs of their lives. The voice of the jazz music is the voice of loneliness in their inner worlds. They express their thoughts, feelings, and emotions without any plan in their movable states. As they travel all around in the United States, they depart from their dissatisfaction in their social environments.

Keywords: Beat Generation, Dis/satisfaction, Traveling, Jazz Music, Alienation.

Introduction

> Someone can wander from city to city, as Kerouac was doing. . . . Jack's desperate flights back and forth across the country during the next six years only mirrored his own confusion.
>
> Ann Charters, *Kerouac: A Biography*

> There was nowhere to go but everywhere, so just keep on rolling under the stars
>
> Jack Kerouac, *On the Road*

As the epigraph notes, Jack Kerouac is a wanderer of various places due to his own confusion in mind. Due to his dissatisfaction because of the sense of loneliness and alienation in his life circumstances, Kerouac has a life on roads. Kerouac highlights individuals' persistence of traveling all around to have freedom through seeing new places in *On the Road*. This signifies that the main character Sal Paradise's, the main character's, travels are a call for "freedom in the frontier West" (Ellis 43). They are a source for relief in their lives. It is significant that the sense of dissatisfaction ends up an epiphany for Paradise in *On the Road*.

As James Joyce expresses, a spiritual awakening rises in Paradise's life when he has dissatisfaction because of loneliness and alienation that directs him to have freedom on roads. As Scholes and Walzl define, "Joyce himself set the pattern for the use of the term epiphany as a spiritual or intellectual apprehension which represented an enlightenment" (252). In *A Portrait of the Artist as a Young Man*, Joyce narrates the experiences of Stephen Dedalus having insight and revelation to become an artist in his life so that he leaves his family and friends back and regards nothing else behind. Thus, it is the spiritual revelation and awakening mind that Joyce states Stephen Dedalus has:

> I will tell you what I will do and what I will not do. I will not serve that in which I no longer believe, whether it calls itself my home, my fatherland, or my church: and I will try to express myself in some mode of life or art as freely as I can and as wholly as I can, using for my defense the only arms I allow myself to use – silence, exile, and cunning. (Joyce 266)

This quotation reflects that he disregards his home, his fatherland, and even his church to travel around. Therefore, he seeks a new life for himself. He aims "to live, to err, to fall, to triumph, to recreate life out of life. A wild angel appeared to him, the angel of mortal youth and beauty, an envoy from the fair courts of life" (Joyce, 186). As this quotation depicts, a new enlightened world view revives Stephen Dedalus. Similarly, Paradise acquires epiphany through wheeling on roads that refresh him and his penniless friends and drive them to have freedom in life.

It is the time to have a reawakening and revelation in the world. This means that he has a time for revelation and enlightenment in his world view. As Elise Ballard notes, epiphanies reveal wisdom and universal truths for individuals to comprehend the significance of real circumstances in their lives (1). At the end of wheeling on roads and hitchhiking, Sal Paradise decides to turn back his home, that is, he revives himself. This signs that the time for revelation and enlightenment emerges for Paradise on roads (Russell 36). He refreshes himself at the end of this world view.

Following his epiphany, Sal Paradise, representing Jack Kerouac, devotes his life for traveling on roads. Leaving everything behind, Paradise concerns what is ahead of him and concerns nothing behind him. He considers that he does not regard his past and he is quite onward. This signifies that traveling on roads has new life for Paradise. This article concurrently concerns the reasons why individuals care about traveling to see different places so that the lack of satisfaction leads them to be on roads.

On the Road is all about young boys' hitchhiking and consists of the reflection of their lives' hardships, sorrows and adventures. The boys are narrating their observations while being on roads where they see "carnivals, lunch carts, factories, farms, all the way over" (*Selected Letters* 170). The book is mainly about the "senses of engagement and alienation; of cultural and personal past; of mythic possibility; of gritty reality; of fantasy, fact, failure, and hope (Hunt 175). This means that a life of traveling hints the existence of hope for Paradise. Wanderings signify a sense of freedom on free ways in the postwar world of 1960s for him (Holton 70). This hints that the road is like an "alternative space of freedom" for Sal (Larson 47). In that case, roads reflect an alive living for him and his friends. Roads express changes within men as Sal expresses in Texas: "Texas, Texas -so you see, man, my soul, the state of things, my position- you notice I get quieter" (Kerouac 230). Silence on roads lies with the self-confidence as in Sal. This emphasizes that he has a new revived atmosphere with new places. Thus, being away from their previous places is a source to refresh their spirits.

The Sense of Dissatisfaction

Sal Paradise has "road-inspired freedom" and becomes a travel-centered individual who concerns new living all around (Larson 35). He emphasizes that he has nothing else but a "life on road." (Kerouac 1). He is restless enough and goes beyond all territories. He defines the "huge world" waiting for him and departs from his conventional past living. Being an individualist because of caring himself, he feels free and self-confident by traveling and defines the meaning of being on roads:

> What is that feeling when you're driving away from people and they recede on the plain till you see their specks dispersing? —It's the too-huge world vaulting us, and it's good-bye. But we lean forward to the next crazy venture beneath the skies. (Kerouac 141)

As the quotation reflects, Sal Paradise is driven by freedom and is interested in all the world. He becomes everyman who goes in other places to have his freedom and departs his previous living (Grace 80). He reflects the hopeful future life existing onward. Kerouac concurrently emphasizes that loneliness and alienation are important thematic matters that cause the sense of dissatisfaction for individuals in the selected novel. He starts the novel having the sense of being a lonely individual. After departing from his wife, his loneliness leads him into having a new friendship: He confronts Dean Moriatry and expresses that he feels seeing the end of everything in his life:

> I first met Dean not long after my wife and I split up. I had just gotten over a serious illness that I won't bother to talk about, except that it had something to do with the miserably weary split-up and my feeling that everything was dead. With the coming of Dean Moriarty began the part of my life you could call my life on the road. (Kerouac 3)

Referring to his life as a "life on the road," Kerouac expresses his free spirit and his alienation from his background. Those thematic issues drive them into moving to see and to be aware of new places. Due to being bored of living in the same circumstances, they reflect their freedom while visiting all around. Through keeping "mobility" by traveling, Paradise hints how he is lonely to wish for his freedom in any case (Cresswell 249). Acquiring a free and happy life by visiting new places is what he and his friends concern. They are interested in having new friendships and wish to see new environments. By visiting all around, they intend to revolt against their state of loneliness and alienation and care for themselves (Watson 3). This means that they are individualistic and consider that new places provide freedom and selfhood to them. Therefore, there is a "quest for the idiosyncratic and often ambivalent identification of selfhood and nostalgia for the security and irresponsibility of childhood in a world that seems to promise only the guarantees of aging and mortality" (Skau 155-156). This emphasizes that they are in a search for finding themselves through going around.

Expressing their selfhood while traveling, Sal Paradise substantially reflects his idiosyncratic identification. He has his sense of confusion because of the senses of alienation and isolation. Traveling to various places signs that they consider themselves as new individuals after every visit. Paradise has a wide perspective to visit new places and spends several years on the road. Then, he writes about his road observations in three weeks: Writing in a short time implies that he has extensive writing subjects (Johnson 28). Therefore, roads symbolize life and become effective for him. He is in a quest for finding new opportunities to lead his life with his travelings. He is concurrently influenced by them psychoanalytically. Concerning other new places implies that a psychoanalytical evaluation explores their traveling as they have a reawakening at the end. Therefore, social reasons for their psychoanalytical changes will be of interest in this article.

Kerouac writes about the Beat Generation in the postwar era of the 1950s in *On the Road*. Beat Generation is simply "the slogan or label for a revolution in manners in America" (Ginsberg-no page number). Therefore, it is a call for freedom in consciousness. In 1948, Kerouac had a conversation with a writer, John Clellon Holmes. After the introduction to a beat (Kerouac), Holmes introduced him and his friends as the Beat Generation in an article for *New York Times Magazine* in 1952. He hinted that "it involves a sort of nakedness of mind, and ultimately, of soul" (Watson 3). The lives of the Beat is significant for Beat literature that can be seen within the works of William Burroughs, Allen Ginsberg, and Jack Kerouac. They have idiosyncratic uncensored narratives about their everyday life (Ibid., 5). It is significant that Beat Generation disregards the conventions and norms (Bailyn 487). What they care is themselves so that nothing else is valuable. Kerouac expresses their protest and becomes "a romantic hero" and "an archetypal rebel, the 1960s symbol of their own vanities, the symbol of their own romantic legend for Beat Generation" (Charters 22). It is significant that Kerouac as a Beat writer has, thereby, a revived psychology. Sal Paradise considers that the road provides life for him (Giamo 20). Thus, he signifies that he revives himself with roads.

It is considerable that while focusing on the Beats, "Kerouac confronted a postwar era neither fitted to modernism nor yet committed to the postmodern"

(Johnson 23) because the Beats are the nonconformists who are dissatisfied with their loneliness in life. Their loneliness drives them to search for finding their freedom in new places. Defining themselves with their feelings and emotions, the Beats express how they marginalize themselves as the Beats. They are under a specific group of people who are on the raod to have self-confidence and freedom in other places:

> The beats, in short, lived both on the road and on the edge. For them, as for pilgrims, transition was a semipermanent condition. . . . . The beats shared, in short, not an identifiable geographical goal but an undefined commitment to a spiritual search. They aimed not to arrive but to travel and, in the process, to transform into sacred space every back alley through which they ambled and every tenement in which they lived their pilgrims, however, was their lack of a "center out there." The beats shared, in short, not an identifiable geographical goal but an undefined commitment to a spiritual search. Thus, the beats appear in their lives and in their novels not only as pilgrims but also as heroes (and authors) of quest tales, wandering (and writing) (Prothero 211)

As the quotation reflects, traveling on roads was their interest. They are in a quest for wandering. They revive themselves while being on roads. To illustrate, Sal Paradise can be accepted as a new person who travels with his friends with whom he has satisfaction when he admires visiting new places in *On the Road*. Similar to him, his penniless young friends become content with the time period, physical beauty, jazz music and even drugs in their lives. They have the sense of loneliness and alienation in their inner worlds. They, thereby, are the "angry young men" (Watson 258). As they travel around, they feel apart from their lack of satisfaction in their livelihood. The music they play, the jazz music, voice their dissatisfaction through their thoughts, feelings, and emotions aloud.

Their traveling through hitching reflect their own inner worlds. They suddenly get in contact with the driver. Similarly, they become strangers in the places they travel. They cannot introduce themselves well in those places. They are haunted by the places they visit and become new individuals because of giving them the sense of freedom. To illustrate, the first quotation in *On the Road* manifests their new identity through their traveling on roads:

> I woke up as the sun was reddening; and that was the one distinct time in my life, the strangest moment of all, when I didn't know who I was—I was far away from home, haunted and tired with travel, in a cheap hotel room I'd never seen, hearing the hiss of steam outside, and the creak of

> the old wood of the hotel, and the footsteps upstairs, and all the sad sounds, and I looked at the cracked high ceiling and really didn't know who I was for about fifteen strange seconds. I wasn't scared; I was just somebody else, some stranger, and my whole life was a haunted life, the life of a ghost. I was halfway across America, at the dividing line between the East of my youth and the West of my future. (Kerouac 16)

As the quotation hints, their differentiation within the time process signs their awareness to become new individuals. They have new experiences and adventures in *On the Road*. It deals with how individuals become aware of new settings through pursuing roads. It depicts about the significance of life and youth: youth consciousness is in utmost significance in life (Swartz 18). The young generation, the Beats, has different life styles. Despite being against the life of loneliness, they continue their pursuit to experience roads. Therefore, they are the happy wanderers who never give up the traveling on roads experience (McKee 5).

Being dissatisfied in their living conditions imply that they are after other ideals in their lives and want to depart their social circumstances. Kerouac depicts a period in which there is the rebellious movement of youth. They conform to the "mass culture" after pursuing a life on the road (Hrebeniak 4). There is a protesting youth against conventional cases such as family life, educational system, military organization, marriage institution, and social life, etc.

Accepted as the classic book of the Beat Generation, *On the Road* is "between truth and artifice" (Theado 53). It depicts how Sal Paradise and Dean evaluate their living environment in realistic terms: They are in loneliness and search for new places to reside to be estranged to their loneliness. Whenever he goes to new place, the psychological distance that he attains becomes longer, because he feels far away from his loneliness as he comes across with new friendships (Ibid., 101). Such an outlook indicates that they are all the time on the road to locate in new places to be far away from loneliness in their new surroundings. They are, thereby, they marginalize themselves for traveling to different places: Thus, they are nonconformists to their original living environments. Therefore, they are in a search for new life in freedom for themselves.

Their new life outlook has American characteristics: They have an "Emersonian and Whitmanian individualism by which one aligns oneself with the marginalized and self-reliant." (Grace 80) They feel themselves to be alienated and lonely. Therefore, they are in a search for finding new friendships in their lives in other locations. They become new individuals in new atmospheres and revive themselves in new environments. They seek for alive social environments and this reflects that they accordingly rebel against their social environment's lifelessness (Kerouac 3). Because of this reason and his "unproductive" college experience, they are in pursuit to travel on roads and acquire detachment from their lifelessness in their social lives. Therefore, they are in a search for lively living. They look for happy social settings and fresh environments. They acquire their individualism while being alone with themselves on roads. They care for attaining new friendships while getting introduced with others. Their concern for having other friendships in other places emphasizes that they are looking for their salvation in the American states and begin for a new life (Theado 57). Having several ideals, Paradise is always movable on roads and feels like a mad man who loses his control in life:

> I stepped right up and gestured in the rain; [...] I looked like a maniac, of course, with my hair all wet, my shoes sopping. My shoes, damn fool that I am, were Mexican huaraches, plantlike sieves not fit for the rainy night of America and the raw road night (Kerouac 12)

Becoming wet in rainy environment, Sal Paradise expresses his unexpected changing emotions. Yet, despite improbable emerging harsh conditions, Paradise is decisive to go on the road. This quotation implies that Paradise decides to move all around in any circumstance. He is adventurous and is leaving his loneliness away as well as trying to search for new places for a happy life. He becomes like a frontier man who is in an escape from immovable surroundings. Therefore, he considers that other individuals are experiencing happy days in their lives in other places. He is innovative and caring for new regions: He is creative enough to have new outlooks.

In his adventurous traveling, Kerouac can be regarded as a modern pilgrim since he cares for visiting other places on the road in contemporary period (Urry 8). He intends to see new environments and have new friendships. They are dissatisfied with their living circumstances and disregard "the middle-class conformity and modernization in post-World War II America." (Bill 397). They become nonconformists to their own social settings and care for other places. Whereas some people in their living process are content with their living opportunities in America, some others like the Beats are not. They consider that their environments are full of "confusion" as well as" nonsense" as Kerouac hints:

> It was drizzling and mysterious at the beginning of our journey. I could see that it was all going to be one big saga of the mist. "Whooee!" yelled Dean. "Here we go!" And he hunched over the wheel and gunned her. . . . . We were all delighted, we all realized we were leaving confusion and nonsense behind, and performing our one and noble function of the time, move. And we moved! We flashed past the mysterious white signs in the night somewhere in New Jersey that say SOUTH (with an arrow) and WEST (with an arrow) and took the south one. New Orleans! It burned in our brains. (Kerouac 120-121)

This quotation manifests why Beat Generation goes away from their own living environments. Confusion and nonsense that they regard in their lives is the main reason for them to prefer going other places to feel relieved. They are delighted while wheeling for other regions. They estimate that moving other distinctions is a noble function. They even look for the nights' mystery. They are interested in the mysterious aspect of entertainment in darkness. They are going for other places to be loyal to their noble function of moving. That is, they are on the road and consider that moving all around is significant for them. (Kerouac 120-121). This signifies that it is their responsibility to travel all around.

Speeding for fresh landscapes is their interest to have new observations that necessitate various transportation means like hitchhiking (Lofgren 61). They concern interesting sides of their visiting environments as Kerouac expresses:

> a trip that was so frantic and so crazy that it has a beginning and an end, began in the heat of the wildest excitement, great jazz, fast driving, women, accidents, arrests, all night movies, and ended all petered out in the dark of Long Island, where we walked a few blocks around my house just because we were so used to moving (Kerouac 350).

Kerouac refers to individuals who have different field of interests. They have utmost excitement for tasting various pursuits: jazz, speedy driving, women, night movies, as well as accidents in addition to arrests. Such kind of entanglements imply that they are fearless and energetic to be active. They express their voice with the jazz music. They are moving to reach new women as well as see new movies at night. They are marginalized due to having a specific life style in freedom. They do not even care about experiencing any accidents and arrests while moving. Freedom becomes like a labyrith for Kerouac that directs him in all country to travel around without deciding any place to arrive (McKee 4).

On the Road is centered on having the perception of seeing various places. Having knowledge at the end of their movement to other places is a means to have new outlooks in life. Individuals reflect how free they are in their attitudes: Nothing can limit their activities of moving to new places. To illustrate, Sal Paradise believes to have good houses in different places. This signifies that all the world is his home:

> Just as we rolled into Iowa City he saw another truck coming behind us, and because he had to turn off at Iowa City . . . . . Now I could see Denver looming ahead of me like the Promised Land, way out there beneath the stars, across the prairie of Iowa and the plains of Nebraska, and I could see the greater vision of San Francisco beyond, like jewels in the night. He balled the jack and told stories for a couple of hours, then, at a town in Iowa where years later Dean and I were stopped on suspicion in what looked like a stolen Cadillac, he slept a few hours in the seat. I slept too, and took one little walk along the lonely brick walls illuminated by one lamp. (Kerouac 14-15)

As the quotation depicts, Sal Paradise accepts different places as new living environment where his home is kept in. All of the places form the Promised Land for him. Yet, they feel anxious in some places: Both Dean and Sal Paradise are in suspicion to possess their happiness in free accommodation. For example, the night is dark and is afraid in itself, however, the night's darkness in itself has other beauties for them. They avoid wasting time while traveling in free spirit. They evaluate everywhere as their homes as the song singing at midnight hints:

> Home in Missoula,
> Home in Truckee,
> Home in Opelousas,
> Ain't no home for me.
> Home in old Medora,
> Home in Wounded Knee,
> Home in Ogallala,
> Home I'll never be (Kerouac 232).

Once they evaluate a place as their home, they concurrently will another place to be their homes. They do not decide which road they are going to follow: Their road direction, at that time, leads them to various places. They are suspicious which road they are going to follow: "What's your road, man? - holy boy road, madman road, rainbow road, guppy road, any road. It's an anywhere road for anybody anyhow. Where body how?" (Kerouac 229). They evaluate it as “madman road” that is suitable for the angry young men of the 1960s. The direction changes according to their sudden decisions and wishes because of being angry young individuals. Their sudden decisions are solely about themselves:

> You have absolutely no regard but yourself and your damned kicks. All you think about is what's hanging between your legs and how much money or fun you can get out of people and then you just throw them aside. Not only that but you're silly about it. It never occurs to you that life is serious and that there are people trying to make something decent out of it instead of just goofing all the time. (Kerouac, 176)

Their freedom to travel around implies that their free spirit leads them to nowhere in mind but everywhere. It is, accordingly, their traveling epic to cross the country. (Kerouac, 2007, 25). They are concurrently free in their friendship choices. Their new friends are the ones who are different than the common individuals:

> the only people that interest me are the mad ones, the ones who are mad to live, mad to talk, desirous of everything at the same time, the ones that never yawn or say a commonplace thing but burn, burn, burn like roman candles across the night.” (Kerouac 7).

Their mad friendships hint that they are angry in their psychological worlds. As Kerouac writes, they are “burning like candles” and light individuals all around. This characteristic attains them angry young characteristic. They choose social individuals who are desirous for everything. They find new friendships in their new houses. Kerouac expresses “his own voice and his true subject” in *On the Road* while traveling (Charters XX). He especially expresses his own voice to Dean Moriatry. He feels himself to be akin to Dean who directs him:

> "Yes! That's right! Wow! Man!" and "Phew!" and wiped his face with his handkerchief. "Man, wow, there's so many things to do, so many things to write! How to even begin to get it all down and without modified restraints and all hung-up on like literary inhibitions and grammatical fears . . ." (Kerouac 6)

Such a dialogue between him and Dean Moriatry reflects how patient he is in his travel decision. In writing, he mainly depicts how he is interested in being active: Therefore, he does not give up seeing new places, new individuals and experiencing new events. They both have joyful and depressive activities through their traveling.

> Then came spring, the great time of traveling, and everybody in the scattered gang was getting ready to take one trip or another. I was busily at work on my novel and when I carne to the halfway mark, after a trip down South with my aunt to visit my brother Rocco, I got ready to travel West for the very first time. (Kerouac 8)

He is ready to travel other places and is interested in seeing new horizons. Being a young writer, he wants to get introduced to new individuals so that he writes as "girls, visions, everything; somewhere along the line the pearl would be handed to me" (Kerouac 10). This explanation hints that he wishes to be an individual who looks for all innovations in his life. People whom he comes across and places he sees inspire him to have a refreshed identity. Therefore, traveling all around departs him from the dissatisfaction of alienation and isolation. Athough he is aware of difficult circumstances, he does not become desperate in his traveling. Therefore, he is determined to attend his departure from his own living circumstances:

> 'You can get a bed but no food. You'll have to eat in town. We travel some.' We thought it over.
>
> 'It's a good opportunity,' he said, and waited patiently for us to make up our minds. We felt silly and didn't know what to say, and I for one didn't want to get hung-up with a carnival. I was in such a bloody hurry to get to the gang in Denver. (Kerouac 20)

Such a dialogue between his friend and himself signifies that they are patient enough for the difficult traveling circumstances. They are decisive enough so that any bad matter will not change their mind to travel. They believe that there are all good opportunities following their paving the ways. Although they are alone on roads and face the confusions (Kerouach 41), they are self-confident while traveling. They go different places on roads: They are going into every different place, because going all around ties them up with everything else. (Kerouac 54). This signs that following different roads refresh them. The flashlights on their ways light their inner psyche and calm them down (Kerouac 57). They always change their residents, because they feel themselves alone in their previous regions. Therefore, they wish to have freedom while going to another place (58). Thereby, Sal Paradise writes about his observations (64) and his writing becomes a means of life for him. Paradise forgives everybody while traveling (70), because he forgets all his back and becomes a new person. Life is settled roads for Sal Paradise and his friends. They do not listen their kins when they warn them because of hanging around:

> I left everybody and went home to rest. My aunt said I was wasting my time hanging around with Dean and his gang. I knew that was wrong, too. Life is life, and kind is kind. What I wanted was to take one more magnificent trip to the West Coast and get back in time for the spring semester in school. And what a trip it turned out to be! I only went along for the ride, and to see what else Dean was going to do, and finally, also, knowing Dean would go back to Camille in Frisco, I wanted to have an affair with Marylou. We got ready to cross the groaning continent again. (Kerouac 116)

This quotation implies that a new life awaits them at the end of their traveling. They are dissatisfied for being tied to a place, so, they look for new places and wish to have new introduction to new individuals. In a way, they refresh themselves.

New friendships mean a new life for them. They all jumped to the music with roads and find purity with them (Kerouac 121). They follow hitchhiking on roads since they do not have any money with them (149). Their own selves are significant for them to earn their lives. They do not regard anything else. They are thinking about getting some money or fun through traveling. This implies that they are significant for themselves to be alive in the world while traveling. They do not regard anybody else but themselves:

> It was time for us to move on. We took a bus to Detroit, Our money was now running quite low. We lugged our wretched baggage through the station. By now Dean's thumb bandage was almost as black as coal and all unrolled. We were both as miserable-looking as anybody could be after all the things we'd done. Exhausted, Dean fell asleep in the bus that roared across the state of Michigan. I took up a conversation with a gorgeous country girl wearing a low-cut cotton blouse that displayed the beautiful sun-tan on her breast tops. She was dull. She spoke of evenings in the country making popcorn on the porch. (Kerouac 220-221)

As the quotation reflects although they are running out of money, they continue their traveling on roads. They go on living the same: taking busses, preparing their baggage, dealing with the girls all around and going bars (Kerouac 235). This signs that they care about their fun and freedom. In addition, Dean's friendship was important for them. Although Dean is like a "frightful Angel," he means the inspiration for life to them.

> Suddenly I had a vision of Dean, a burning shuddering frightful Angel, palpitating toward me across the road, approaching like a cloud, with

> enormous speed, pursuing me like the Shrouded Traveler on the plain, bearing down on me. I saw his huge face over the plains with the mad, bony purpose and the gleaming eyes; I saw his wings; I saw his old jalopy chariot with thousands of sparking flames shooting out from it; I saw the path it burned over the road; it even made its own road and went over the corn, through cities, destroying bridges, drying rivers. It came like wrath to the West. I knew Dean had gone mad again. (Kerouac 236)

They are travelers in unity with their friendships. They are not alone when they are traveling together. They have their freedom on roads and, yet, they have their own madness through their actions and behaviours. They are happy as they face their own excessive actions.

> Yass, well-we're all together now and the years have rolled severally behind us and yet you see none of us have really changed, that's what so amazing, the dura-the dura-bility-in fact to prove that I have here a deck of cards with which I can tell very accurate fortunes of all sorts. . . . . Dean suddenly grew quiet and sat in a kitchen chair between Stan and me and stared straight ahead with rocky doglike wonder and paid no attention to anybody. (Kerouac 239)

They have "doglike wonder" so that their curiosity does not regard anybody else but solely themselves. In new places, they have new friendships through traveling and try to have fun there. They become really curious individuals:

> 'Are we gonna get our kicks, Sal, traveling down to Mexico with this cat Stan! Yes!' It was our last night in holy Denver, we made it big and wild. It all ended up with wine in the basement by candlelight, and Charity creeping around upstairs in her nightgown with a flashlight. We had a colored guy with us now, called himself Gomez. He floated around Five Points and didn't give a damn. (Kerouac 240-241)

They have fun through going into the bars in Denver at their last night. They have their new introductions to new individuals there. Their curiosity is a life source for them. Sal takes the wheel thereby and drives to Fredericksburg. After Denver, Sal is in England: London to Liverpool he is having adventures through new hitchhiking. He is having the voices of Europe while traveling (Kerouac 246-247). Later, Dean takes the wheel to dive into San Antonio. They go into "town in a wilderness of Mexican rickety southern shacks without cellars and with old rocking chairs on the porch" and stop at a gas station (Kerouac 247). While traveling, they are introduced to the world:

> 'It's the world! We can go right on to South America if the road goes. Think of it! Son-of-z-bitch! Gawd-damm!' We rushed on. The dawn spread immediately and we began to see the white sand of the desert and occasional huts in the distance off the road (Kerouac 252).

They are awakened with roads as Kerouac expresses through Dean. The world becomes meaningful for them and they get interested with the world. There is no distance among themeselves as they go on traveling:

> 'Hee! Wheel Hoo!' yelled Dean. He was wide awake and jumping up and down in that drowsy Mexican street. 'Let's all go!' I was passing Lucky Strikes to the other boys. They were getting great pleasure out of us and especially Dean. They turned to one another with cupped hands and rattled off comments about the mad American cat. 'Dig them, Sal, talking about us and digging. Oh my goodness, what a world!' Victor got in the car with us, and we lurched off. Stan Shephard had been sleeping soundly and woke up to this madness. (Kerouac 256)

While turning to each other, they are getting pleasure for living in the world. They are aware of having goodness in the world and wake up at the end of their madness. Sal expresses having the sense of reality in this life when he feels he wakes up as if from "void to a dream:"

> For a long time I lost consciousness in my lower mind of what we were doing and only came around sometime later when I looked up from fire and silence like waking from sleep to the world, or waking from void to a dream, and they told me we were parked outside Victor's house and he was already at the door of the car with his little baby son in his arms, showing him to us. (Kerouac 260)

He is having his consciousness as if waking from sleeping to experiencing the real world. He becomes well aware of the voice of the real world and leaves all silent living behind. Instead of losing conscience, he is well awakened to be aware of living in the new world. Sal becomes a new person in his life at the end of traveling to different places. Moreover, he decides to go his home back:

> In the fall I myself started back home from Mexico City and one night just over Laredo border in Dilley, Texas, I was standing on the hot road underneath an arc-lamp with the summer moths smashing into it when I heard the sound of footsteps from the darkness beyond, and lo, a tall old man with flowing white hair came clomping by with a pack on his back, and when he saw me as he passed, he said, 'Go moan for man,' and clomped on back to his dark. Did this mean that I should at last go on my

> pilgrimage on foot on the dark roads around America? I struggled and hurried to New York, and one night I was standing in a dark street in Manhattan and called up to the window of a loft where I thought my friends were having a party. (210)

As this quotation reflects, Sal is on his pilgrimage on foot so that he recognizes most places through going around various places. He is in search for all the world through being on roads. He is searching to have new friendships. Dark streets become well lighted when he passes them and he is aware of them. New friends become new life for him. As Newhouse underlines:

> Sal Paradise ….. embraces the mysteries and excesses of life provided by trips to Mexico, San Francisco, Los Angeles, Denver and New York. In these settings the novel moves away from areas that are systematically stifling—from east to West, from civilized to primitive—and it is within more remote environments that primal connection and strangeness are seen as promising vehicles to psychic and spiritual recovery. (58)

Traveling is a recovery for Sal so that he becomes a new individual full of life in his spirit. He faces modern civilizations and forgets all about his previous living. New horizons are all embracing him in various places like Mexico, San Francisco, Los Angeles, Denver and New York. As much as Sal Paradise travels and recognizes new places, the new regions become familiar to him, therefore, he requires to reach other places.

Conclusion

Sal Paradise, who begins to feel distant from the environment he lives in, chooses to travel on the roads as a new behavior in *On the Road*. In this way, he gives himself a way of liberation and relaxation. He wants to meet new people and learn about their cultures by traveling on the roads. New people also bring him new friendships and become a source of life.

Sal Paradise, a member of the Beat Generation, is constantly looking for new places to go. He goes to various places by hitchhiking and makes friends with many people. Traveling gives him the opportunity to renew himself. Re-awakened, Paradise now feels like a new person. Gaining the sense of liberation is a great feature he has gained.

Acquired by a sense of dissatisfaction, Paradise explores new places and tries ways to please himself. Every place is a new gain and joy of life for him. A place is a way of self-knowledge in Paradise. As he gets to know himself, he lives happily around him. The tensions he experiences imply the complex environment he feeds within himself. Any tension that ends well reminds him of the peaceful world in which he will eventually live. He emphasizes the financial difficulties he experienced during his travels and the troubles of the people around him. The disappearance of every economic crisis implies that people have freed themselves from financial distress. Now they feel well, thus, it reminds them how much their psychological structures are affected by the economic structure. In these times of trouble, people need support. Every received support will be a sign of endless friendships formed in social life. Sal Paradise makes you feel that these friendships are essential on your trips. His friendship with Dean demonstrates this aspect. This shows that the basis of friendships is the material and moral support. As you travel to different places, those places become familiar. Finally, Sal Paradise wants to see new places and meet new people. Undesirable unrest in his own living area, where he lived before, disturbed him. In this case, it was his greatest desire to get away from this dissatisfaction and go on a journey.

Bibliography

Bailyn, Bernard. *The Great Republic: A History of the American People.* Lexington: D. C. Heath and Company, 1992.

Ballard, Elise. "Introduction: What is Your Greatest Epiphany in Life." *Epiphany.* 1-14. New York: Random House, 2011.

Bill, Roger. "Traveller or Tourist? Jack Kerouac and the Commodification of Culture." *Dialectical Antropology.* September 2010. (34): 3. 2010: 395-417, https://www.jstor.org/stable/29790956.

Charters, Ann. "Introduction." *On the Road.* Penguin Books. 2000: vii-ixxx

Charters, Ann. *A Bibliography of Works by Jack Kerouac.* New York: Phoenix Bookshop, 1975.

Cresswell, Tim. "Mobility as Resistance: A Geographical Reading of Kerouac's *On the Road.*" *Transactions of the Institute of British Geographers.* (18): 2. 1993: 249-262. https://www.jstor.org/stable/pdf/622366.pdf.

Ellis, R. J. "I'm only a Jolly Storyteller: Jack Kerouac's *On the Road* and Visions of Cody." *The Beat Generation Writers.* Ed. Robert Lee. Connecticut: Lumiere Press Ltd. and Pluto Press. 1996: 37-61.

Holton, Robert. "The Tenement Castle: Kerouac's Lumpen-Bohemia." *Critical Essays on* On the Road, Eds. Hilary Holladay and Robert Holton. Carbondale: Southern Illinois University, 2009: 60-77.

Hrebeniak, Michael. *Action Writing: Jack Kerouac's Wild Form.* Carbondale: Southern Illinois University Press, 2006.

Hunt,Tim. "Typetalking: Voice and Performance in On the Road." *Critical Essays on* On the Road. Eds. Hilary Holladay and Robert Holton. Carbondale: Southern Illinois University. 2009: 169-187.

Giamo, Ben. (2000). "Kerouac, the Word and the Way: Prose Artist as Spiritual Quester." Carbondale: Southern Illinois University Press.

Ginsberg, Allen. *The Best Minds of My Generation: A Literary History of the Beats*. New York: The Estate of Allen Ginsberg, 2017.

Grace, Nancy. M. "The Quest—Part I: On the Road." *Jack Kerouac and the Literary Imagination.* New York: Palgrave Macmillian, 2007.

Hendry, Irene. "Joyce's Epiphanies" *The Sewanee Review.* Vol. 54. No. 3. 1946: 449-467. http://www.jstor.com/stable/27537675.

Johnson, Joyce. "Kökeninden Kopuş." *Jack Kerouac'ın Yalnız Hayatı: Anlatım Her Şeydir.* (*The Voice is All: The Lonely Victory of Jack Kerouac*). Aydın Çavdar, Trans. İstanbul: Ayrıntı Publications, 2017.

Johnson, Ronna. C. "You're Putting Me on: Jack Kerouac and the Postmodern Emergence." *Teaching Beat Literature.* (27): 1. The Johns Hopkins University Press, 2000: 22-38 https://www.jstor.org/stable/2511249

Joyce, James. *A Portrait of the Artist as a Young Man*. İstanbul: Sis Publishing, 2013.

Kerouac, Jack. *On the Road.* London: Penguin Books, 2000.

Kerouac, Jack. *On the Road.* New York: Library: The Library of America, 2007.

Kerouac, Jack. *Selected Letters: 1940–1956.* Ed. Ann Charters. New York: Viking. 1995.

Larson, Lars Eric. "Free Ways and Straight Roads: The Interstates of Sal Paradise and 1950s America." *Critical Essays an Jack Kerouac's* On the Road. Eds. Hilary Holladay and Robert Holton. Southern Illinois University, 2009.

Lofgren, Orvar. *On Holiday: A History of Vacationing.* Berkeley: University of California Press, 1999.

McKee, Jenn. *Great Writers: Jack Kerouac.* Philadephia: Chelsea House Publishers, 2004.

Newhouse, Thomas. *The Beat Generation and the Popular Novel in the United States, 1945-1979.* North Carolina: McFarland and Company, Inc. Publishers, 2000.

Prothero, Stephen. "On the Holy Road: The Beat Movement as Spiritual Protest." *The Harvard Theological Review.* (84): 2. Cambridge University Press, 1991: 205-222. https://www.jstor.org/stable/1509800

Russell, Brian. "James Joyce: Prospects for Epiphany." 1993. https://journals.sagepub.com/doi/abs/10.1177/0040571X9309600105?journalCode=tjxa.

Scholes, Robert. and Florence L. Walzl. "The Epiphanies of Joyce." *PMLA*. Vol. 82. No. 1. 152-154. https://www.jstor.org/stable/461060. 1967.

Skau, M. "The Makings of Paradise?" *Critical Essays on* On the Road, Hilary Holladay and Robert Holton. Eds. Carbondale: Southern Illinois University, 2009: 155-169.

Swart, O. *The View from* On the Road. Carbondale: Southern Illinois State University Press, 1999.

Theado, Matt. *Understanding Jack Kerouac*. Columbia: University of South Caroline Press. 2000.

Urry, Jhon. "The Tourist Gaze: Leisure and Travel in Contemporary Societies." London: Sage Publications, 1997.

Watson, Steven. *The Birth of the Beat Generation: Visionaries. Rebels, and Hipsters, 1944-1960*. New York: Phanteon Books, 1995.

A Short Bio of Assoc. Prof. Dr. Zennure KÖSEMAN

Assoc. Prof. Dr. Zennure Köseman is in Inonu University. Her BA is from English Language and Literature Department in Hacettepe University. She has her MA from History Department in Bilkent University focusing on American, British and Ottoman histories. She holds her Ph.D. from Hacettepe University American Culture and Literature Department.

The Author's Awareness of Her Own Author Identity at the Crossroad of Travelogue and Memoir: Agatha Christie's *Come, Tell Me How You Live*

Assoc. Prof. Dr. Mevlüde ZENGİN

Abstract

Travel writings are the works comprised in non-imaginative literature due to their dependence on the actual life. In the western world, people wrote travelogues abundantly owing to the travels and expeditions specifically in the 18th and 19th centuries. However, critical studies on travel writings began to be a prolific area of study especially in the second half of the 20th century and in the century we are living in. Agatha Christie's *Come, Tell Me How You Live: An Archeological Memoir* is a travel writing she wrote after she and her husband, Max Mallowan travelled to Syria due to his archeological explorations between 1930-1938. Written about four years after the travels, the book depends on Christie's memories. Therefore, it will not be wrong to call it a travel memoir. The purpose of this study is to put forward the ideas that Christie wrote her book with an awareness of her being a fiction writer and it contains many implications and instances of the reflection of Christie's own identity as an author. To this end, the study focuses on firstly, Christie's constructing her book, secondly, the strategies in her narration, thirdly, the style and tone, fourthly, her use of language and lastly, themes in *Come, Tell Me How You Live*. The final remark of the study is that Christie wrote her book benefiting from her ability of writing fiction; and this makes *Come, Tell Me How You Live* a book close to fiction and an enjoyable book giving the reader pleasure of reading with its fiction-like aspects.

Keywords: Identity, Memoir, Fiction, Archeological Explorations, Non-imaginative literature

Introduction

Although travelogues, the writings within the scope of non-imaginative literature, were proliferated with the increase in travels, trips and voyages and research opportunities in the western world especially in the 18th and 19th centuries, travel literature studies have begun to gain importance only in the second half of the 20th century and at the beginning of the 21st century; and as a result of this interest in travel writings, they have appeared as a different field of study in academia. Travel literature studies have become increasingly important in academia in recent years due to the fact that travel writings are inherently prolific, protean and flourishing. Therefore, travel writings have either been studied individually or are used as a secondary source in the scrutinies of other studies. Travel writings' nature of being prolific and diverse owes much to its encompassing other genres in non-fiction — based on the real lives of real people — such as diary, journal, memoir, expedition writings or exploration reports and the like. Agatha Christie's *Come, Tell Me How You Live* (1946) is a work written after both Christie and her archeologist husband Sir Max Mallowan had archeological trips in the Middle East in 1930. The work can be defined as a book between a travel writing and a memoir because it includes the factual information about the archaeological trips and diggings and the memories and remembrances Christie had after these trips, explorations and findings. Therefore, it would not be wrong to call the book as a travel memoir rather than just a travelogue or just a memoir. This study aims to handle *Come, Tell Me How You Live* to detect the ways that Agatha Christie, the writer of detective stories par excellence, adopted in her narrative and that prove Christie's awareness of her own author identity. Such an exploration may be interesting when considering the fact that travelogues and memoirs, like most of the other genres in non-imaginative literature, do not need to be written by professional or full-time writers; that is, they may also be written by a number of occasional writers. The works written by professional authors such as Christie and those written by occasional writers having other professions such as scientists, doctors, explorers, diplomats, scholars, missionaries, soldiers, politicians and sailors may have important differences in many respects the likes of the construction of the work, language and narrative strategies employed in the work as well as the intention of the author. Yet, this study does not aim to present a comparative examination between Christie's book and a travel memoir written by an unprofessional writer. The main purpose of this study is to reflect the ideas that Christie wrote *Come, Tell Me How You Live* with an awareness that she was a great writer and that the book contains many implications and instances of the reflection of Christie's own identity as an author. Furthermore, during the reading of the book, as readers, we always feel that the book was not written by an occasional writer in order to inform the readers about the travels, expreriences and memories of the author; rather it was written by a professional writer in order to reflect the memorable parts of her travels in a work of non-fiction yet in a fiction-like book. For this reason, Christie's book presents the reader with a pleasure of reading by creating a feeling that the book is not only an informative travel account or just a memoir but a text containing many memories gained during travels and expressed in a literary language and style and focusing on the author's life and her experiences in the course of time chosen. Thus, the book can also be defined as an autofictional text, during the reading of which the reader has a pleasure of reading both an autobiographical writing such as travelogues and memoirs, and fiction. Meantime, it should be noted that Christie published the book under the name Agatha Christie Mallowan. It is because her wish to distance her book from her crime fiction "as she did it with some of her romantic fiction" (Campbell, 2005: 97). We know that when Christie wrote *Come, Tell Me How You Live*, she was a famous author of detective fiction. Taking this as a point of departure, in this study, the book will be scrutinized with respect to how Christie benefited from her authorship and reflected her talent as an accomplished writer while writing her travel memoir. In effect, Christie does not touch on her carreer as a best-selling novelist of detective fiction in the book. Yet the analysis offered by this study is thought to be valuable in the context of non-fiction. Although Christie mentions her work in a humble way and says that it is "a light-hearted frivolous book" containing "so many little silly things" (500), this study explores Christie's ways of constructing her work, her employment of narrative strategies, the style and tone, her use of language along with some thematic qualities in *Come, Tell Me How You Live* in order to indicate the author's awareness of her own authorship while writing the book and that Christie benefited from a series of elements of fiction the likes of plot, characterization, style, tone and theme.

I. Agatha Christie's Construction of *Come, Tell Me How You Live*

Before examining *Come, Tell Me How You Live* in respect of its construction, it would be better to give a bit of general information about the book and its reception in its own time. The information about *Come, Tell Me How You Live* that Agatha Christie provided in her *Autobiography* enlightens one's understanding of when and why she wrote this book. She writes:

> I was to make one more variation from my usual literary work. I wrote a book out of nostalgia, because I was separated from Max, could so seldom get news of him, and recalled with such poignant remembrance the days we had spent in Arpachiyah and in Syria. I wanted to re-live our life, to have the pleasure of remembering — and so I wrote *Come, Tell Me How You Live.* (Christie 500)

In an earlier part of her *Autobiography*, Christie states that she wrote the book to recall those good old days in Syria and that her book is a pleasurable one:

> During the Second World War, when I was working in London, I wrote an account of our time in Syria. I called it *Come, Tell Me How You Live,* and I get pleasure in reading it over from time to time, and remembering our days in Syria. One year on a dig is very like another – the same sort of things happen — so repetition would not avail much. They were happy years, we enjoyed ourselves immensely, and had a great measure of success in our digging. (Christie 466-467)

Christie calls her book a "meandering chronicle" in the dedication part of the book[1] and "not a profound book" but "a very little book, full of everyday doings and happenings" (18) in the "Foreword" of the book. She gives, in effect, an account of the daily doings and common chores in her book. As Christie remarks in the above extract, the days during archeological trips and excavations were monotonous. Yet, it can be said that being conscious enough about what she could do in order not to bore the reader and how she could make her book an enjoyable one for the reader, Christie seems to have avoided recurrences in the book. In order to avoid recurrences, she gave the accounts of very specific events that made their days special; in other words, the book offers selective glimpses into their lives and archeological explorations in the Middle East. Even if she had to write about the monotony of the days, it is expressed in a concise manner in order not to bore the reader. Thus reading this book becomes a pleasure for the reader.

The author also conveys the reader the information about a friend's and her publishers' rejection of the publication of *Come, Tell Me How You Live* because they thought that the readers would not like the book and it would not sell well as it is not a detective story. But Christie foreseeing the things and thinking that people would like this amusing book, which was produced out of

---

[1] Christie Mallowan, Agatha. *Come, Tell Me How You Live: An Archeological Memoir.* (United Kingdom: Harper Collins, Inc., 1999), p. 4. (All future references will be to this edition and only page numbers will be given within parentheses in the text.)

the nostalgia for the days she spent with her husband Max Mallowan — because during the WWII, they had to depart from each other for a long time — , opposed their rejection and insisted on its publication although the book was different from her serious detective stories she had previously written. Then Christie tells us that it was a success (2010: 500-501).

Come, Tell Me How You Live is a book giving insight into some of Christie's novels having an orientalist setting. It is known that Christie wrote her novels having stories depicting the East and Eastern people such as *Murder in Mesopotamia* and *Appointment with Death* with the inspiration she took from the life in those exotic places in the East. Her biographer Charles Osborne (1999) gives the contents of *Come, Tell Me How You Live* as in the following:

> The details of life on the digs is brought to life admirably by Agatha Christie in *Come, Tell Me How You Live*, which she was not to publish until 1946, although she began keeping a diary in Syria, with a view to expanding her notes eventually into a book. The life suited her. Max would depart every morning at dawn to work at the mound, and on most days Agatha would accompany him, though occasionally she would stay at home to deal with various chores. There was pottery to be mended, there were objects to be labelled, and of course there was usually an Agatha Christie novel to be created on the typewriter (152).

The above extract clearly gives one the idea that the eastern life and world gave inspiration to Christie during the writing of her aforementioned novels. Her *Come, Tell Me How You Live* with its oriental setting may be thought to be a book that constituted the basis for her novels with oriental setting. With its realistic picture of the Oriental, the book may also be helpful for the readers reading her oriental novels.

I.1. The beginning of the book:

Come, Tell Me How You Live begins with a dedication to Christie's husband and the Colonel, Bumps, Mac and Guilford, who accompanied the Mallowans in their expedition and excavations. Then Christie put a map showing Syria and Mesopotamia. The map also shows the eastern part of Turkey and The Mediterranean Sea partially as well as those countries as Iraq, Lebanon, Palestine and Jordan. It is apparent that this aims to inform the reader unfamiliar with those places. The book's including a map may be seen as a significant aspect of the travel writings. When the places are referred to throughout the book, the reader can have a look at the map(s) in order to understand the route of the travellers or the explorers and see, on the map, the real geographical places they travel. Christie has benefited from this feature of travelogues.

Then it is observed that Christie wrote a ten stanza poem titled "A-sitting On A Tell", which contains the line "Come, tell me how you live!", which Christie employed as the title of her book. Campbell suggests that "the title is a pun — 'tell' is Arabic for a mound or hill formed by a buried archaeological site" (97). The title containing a pun may be considered to imply Christie's profession as a writer. To return to the poem, the whole text of Christie's poem was taken from Lewis Carroll's poem, "A-sitting On A Gate", which first appeared, in 1871, in his novel *Through the Looking Glass*, which is the sequel to *Alice's Adventures in Wonderland.* The poem is given in the novel in the form of a ballad sung by the Knight whom Alice met and it is assumed to be accompanied by music (Carroll 245-248). Christie's poem is actually an adaptation of Carroll's poem with slight differences in some words and expressions. Christie followed the structure of Carroll's poem closely and wrote her "A-sitting On A Tell". Changing some words and parts of the poem slightly, Christie transformed it into a poem, the subject matter of which is archeology. Probably because she changed Carroll's poem partially on the word level, Christie apologizes from the poet with a paranthetical expression put just after the title of the poem.

In order to elaborate on the changes in the poem, the first stanzas of both Carroll's and Christie's poems may be referred to. Carroll's first stanza goes:

> I'll tell thee everything I can:
> There's little to relate.
> I saw an aged aged man,
> A-sitting on a gate.
> "Who are you, aged man?" I said,
> "And how is it you live?"
> And his answer trickled through my head,
> Like water through a sieve. (Carroll 245)

And Christie's first stanza goes:

> I'll tell you everything I can
> If you will listen well:
> I met an erudite young man
> A-sitting on a Tell.
> "Who are you, sir?" to him I said,
> "For what is it you look?"
> His answer trickled through my head
> Like bloodstains in a book. (9)

It is observed that Chrisite adapted Carroll's verse, substituting the word "tell" for "gate" which suggests an archeological site or a mound. In Carroll's case, an aged man sitting on a gate is asked who he is and how he earns his living but in Christie's "an erudite young man" sitting on a tell is asked the first same question and what he is looking for. In Carroll's verse, the answer "trickled through" the speaking personae's head is "like water through a sieve"; Christie's erudite young man's answer trickled through is "like bloodstain in a book, which suggests the idea that Christie refers to her crime novels.

As a conclusion, we can say that the intertextual practice between Lewis and Christie's poems served Christie to start her book.

I.2. The reason for the use of Lewis Carroll's poem "A-Sitting on A Gate":

Christie's transformed poem seems to be used as an epigraph or preface indicating that archeology would be the subject matter in the book. Besides, the line "Come, tell me how you live!" was not exposed to any change; it was taken from Carroll's poem as it was. This indicates that Christie was inspired by this line not only to give her book a title but also to find a point of departure for her book.

Then in the "Foreword" Christie explains the reason for writing this book saying that the book is a response to frequently asked questions such as what they did in Syria and how they lived there. The author seems to have combined these and similar questions that were asked to them and the question that, she supposes, is asked by archeology. "It is the question", she writes "that Archeology asks of the Past — *Come, tell me how you lived*?" (17). So she seems to have used the line "Come, tell me how you live!" for her own purpose: to explain the aim or scope of archeology as a science and to constitute a logical beginning for her book.

I. 3. The Formation of the book in parts, each of which has a title:

Come, Tell Me How You Live is a book which comprises a prologue, twelve chapters and an epilogue. While the prologue and epilogue do not bear particular titles, the twelve parts, by which Christie gives detailed information about their excursions, workings during the excavations and the life they lived in Syria, have titles, each of which gives an idea about what the part is primarily about. The titles "A Surveying Trip", "Journey's End" and "Arriving of Mac" exemplify this. In two of the titles, Christie preferred to use French; "1. Partant pour la Syrie" meaning "Travel to Syria" and "5. Fin de Saison" meaning "The End of the Season". In some of the titles, some real name places were contained; for example, "3. The Habur and the Jaghjagha" , "7. Life at Chagar Bazar" and "10. The Trail to Raqqa". The title of the last chapter is "12. 'Ain el' Arus", which is a Syrian village.

Christie's way of constructing her book via chapters gives one the idea that it helped the author organize the book in the way that she could give their experiences in a chronological order and helped the reader understand what each chapter contains and read them without confusion. In this regard, Christie seems to have benefited from her ability as a novelist to construct a book and create an order among the things she wanted to depict in her book and give them in an ordered and logical way. Just like a novelist of a traditional-realistic novel who creates a linear plot structure and puts the incidents in the plot in an order, Christie gives an account of happenings and situations containing their experiences in the order of their occurences. However, it was Christie herself who decided which event would be told and which event would precede or come after which event in the book and etc.

The book's inclusion of some photographs is also an aspect of the travelogues, which Christie benefited from. The author included some photographs of the people she mentioned in the book, taken while either working or posing for the photograph. Between the pages 128 and 129, there are sixteen photographs illustrating people, places, excavations, vehicles used during trips and even water-carrying donkey.

I. 4. Characterization in the book:

Characterization is a literary device suggesting the creation, introduction and depiction of all characters in a work of fiction. It is used step by step in a literary work to highlight and explain the details about characters. Although *Come, Tell Me How You Live* is a work based on real incidents and characters, Christie did not neglect, in her book, to employ characterization which is an important element in fiction. This paves the way for the book's literariness and pretending as a fictional work.

Christie's book is a very crowded book containing many people from different nationalities such as Arabs, Turks, Armenians, Kurds and Yezidi. What attracts the reader's attention about their portrayal is that Christie drew these people with their funniest sides. She even makes fun of both herself and her husband. Thus she recreates them in comic situations in her book. Yet, Christie drew them realistically refers to them with their proper names. Among these people are Mac (the architect), Hamoudi (the foreman), M. Seyrig, Abdullah, Aristide (the driver), 'Isa, Baron von Oppenheim, Yahya and Alawi (Hamoudi's sons), Abd es Salaam (the other foreman), Michel (the chauffeur), Abdul Aziz, Subri, Mansur, Saleh Birro, Ferhid, Dimitri (the cook), Serkis and Guilford. Salespersons, taxi drivers, conductors, Turkish Customs officials, the postmaster, the hotel owners, travellers, French ladies, the French Lieutenant, the French military officers, the Sheikh and his wives, the Colonel, workers on the excavations, Kurdish men and women, basket-boys and many others are the people who appear in various scenes throughout the book. What is interesting about all these people is that Christie remembered them after years during the writing of her book and referring to them in the relevant scenes through sometimes their outward appearances, sometimes their manners and behaviours, sometimes their speeches, sometimes their relationships with each other and sometimes their reactions. Osborne's (1999) description of Christie's attitudes toward her characters in the book is heplful to understand the characterization in the book:

> The Mallowan team of regulars were clearly agreeable, interesting and amusing people to be with, and Mrs Mallowan's stores of the Arab workmen, the Turks and the desert Sheikhs are colourful, lively, and occasionally touching and thought-provoking (258).

Christie does not only present her readers with a brilliant characterization but an attractive picture of Agatha Christie herself. She reveals her many personal traits. As the author and the narrator of the book, Christie deservingly reveals herself as an intelligent, wise, sensible, witty, industrious, helpful, foreseeing and a learned person who is a good observant and open to learning. Endurance, trying to overcome hardships and never giving up are her other personal traits. She is also a person who can easily adjust the unfamiliar environments, situations and lives.

II. Agatha Christie's Narratological Strategies in *Come, Tell Me How You Live*

II. 1. The narrative method in the book:

Come, Tell Me How You Live naturally employs the first-person narrator owing to its autobiographical quality. Christie as a speaker in the book functions like an author-narrator in fiction. She gives the accounts of either her own experiences as the person taking part in the events or of the other people's experiences as a person witnessing the incidents and situations. Although the whole book relies on external realities and gives the reader what is seen and what is heard, Christie gives her own ideas, insights, feelings and emotions about the incidents occurring, people met and places gone. Therefore, it can be said that the employment of the first-person narrator provides the reader with the unseen and unheard personal ideas and emotions, especially those of the author employed as a first-person narrator. This aspect of *Come, Tell Me How You Live* will be exemplified in the following part dealing with the subjectivity of the author.

The use of free indirect speech, which is a technique in fiction, is also impressive in the book though there are not many. In order to exemplify it, Christie's presenting the Sheikh's voice partly mediated by her own voice can be given. Christie transmits his speech, without using the main clause or an introductory expression, in just subordinate clause. In the last sentence of the following extract, Christie conveys the Sheik's words directly: "The Sheikh quickly gives up the idea of a touch and explains that he has a dear friend and relation outside who has a bad eye. *Will we come out and look at it and advise*?(emphasis is mine) (128). The situation proceeds and then we are told that "the Sheikh nods. His friend is going into Alep. *Will we give him a letter to Dr. Altounyan there?*" (emphasis is mine) (128). Another instance can be found in the scene where Michel is in a troublesome situation:

> Michel now returns, reports that the watchman he has been sent to transport to the mound has three wives, eight children, many sacks of flour and rice, and a good deal of livestock. *Impossible to transport them all in the lorry. What shall he do?* (emphasis is mine) (138).

In both examples, Christie as a narrator speaks through the other persons's mouths in the italicized parts.

Generally written in the present tense, *Come, Tell Me How You Live* presents its readers a unique story-telling style. One who reads a few travelogues or memoirs observes that as these are the accounts of past events, journeys, experiences and memories, they are generally written down in the simple past tense. Even in many novels, due to the assumption that the experiences of the main character occured in the past, either a third person narrator or a first person narrator (especially in the traditional-realistic novels) tells the story in the past tense; that is, the tense by which the narrative is told is usually the simple past tense when a past action is referred to and the past form of "to be" is used when a situation in the past is suggested. In contrast with the often seen ways of story-telling, Christie employs simple present when an action is told and "to be" in present as an ordinary verb to denote the existences of things and people and to express their conditions. From the beginning till the end of the book, it is apparent that the present tenses were used to express particular events that occurred even once. We should also note that, in this way, Christie found out the way to describe the events, which happened many times during their life at different times and archaeological excavations in Syria, in one go. However, during her narrative in the present tense, Christie occasionally used the past tense to express the events that took place in the past and the present perfect to express recently completed actions, considering the time she was in. But the expressions in past and perfect tenses do not bulk large in the book. The author used mostly the present tense. Among numberless examples for the use of present tense to express a past action, as if it were occuring at present, we can give Christie's following expressions: "In the midst of chaos, however, our cook (a new cook, Dimitri by name) continues calmly to prepare an evening meal. We set to and eat with relish, and after that we retire to bed worn out (80). Immediately after this expression, Christie reflects her restlessness due to the mouse in her bedroom by using the present perfect tense to express a recently past experience of hers: "I have never been one with an exaggerated distaste for mice. An odd mouse or so in a bedroom has left me unmoved" (80). In another scene of the book, while talking about rescuing their car that got stuck in the mud, the author uses past and perfect tenses to express actions occuring recently: "Today has been memorable for a rescue. There was rain in the night, and this morning the ground was still soggy. About twelve o'clock a wild-looking horseman arrived, riding with the wildness and desperation of one who brings the good news from Aix to Ghent, etc." (154) . When she returns to present (this may be called 'implied past' because Christie actually refers to past in present; we all know that *Come, Tell Me How You Live* contains Christie's memories), Christie again uses present tense: "Actually he brings bad news [...] The horseman is sent back once with two spades, and we fit out a rescue party in Poilu. Five men go with Serkis in charge. They take spades and extra boards and depart very gaily, singing!" (154).

By the employment of the present tense in her book to give an account of past events, Christie, experimenting with the narrative time(s), both created a narrative style, which is ahead of its time and also gave the sense of a dramatic narrative. This distinguishes the book from travelogues and memoirs having usual narrative styles, and also giving the reader the feeling that the author is describing an action in a story or a play. This makes the narrative of the book both interesting and entertaining for the reader.

II. 2. Subjectivity of the author in the book:

As has already been mentioned in the above part, *Come, Tell Me How You Live* has inherently the perspective of the first-person narrator as it is an autobiographical work. Benefiting from the advantage of the first-person narration, Christie tells us her own inner ideas and emotions which she did not reveal the persons around her. Namely, in some situations she does not reveal her ideas about the situation or the people taking part in the action; rather, she conveys the ideas she had in her mind and feelings in her inner world to the reader only. Therefore, the reader gets Christie's ideas, insights and feelings by means of the subjectivity presented in the work.

While narrating a memory, Christie says that she got nervous at his short answers to everything when she just met Macd, the architect and when she did not know him well. She remembers her own shyness in her youthful age. She shares her inner ideas about her own shyness with the reader. The revelation of her feelings can be found in the following extract:

> I find myself somewhat damped. An uneasy conviction sweeps over me that our young architect is going to prove one of those people who from time to time succeed in rendering me completely imbecile with shyness. I have, thank goodness, long left behind me the days when I was shy of everyone. I have attained, with middle age, a fair amount of poise and savoir faire. Every now and then I congratulate myself that all that silly business is over and done with! 'I've got over it,' I say to myself happily. And as surely as I think so, some unexpected individual reduces me once more to nervous idiocy (33).

In another scene of the book, Christie, without revealing anybody, even Max, her longing for civilization, reflects them as her ideas in her mind. She says: "Approaching civilization stirs within me. I begin to think of things. …A shampoo, a luxurious drier. Manicure. … A porcelain bath with taps. Bath salts. Electric light. … More shoes!" (183).

III. The Style and Tone in Come, Tell Me How You Live

III.1. Christie's focus on the external details and her realism in the book:

The book offers many detailed descriptions of people, events, situations and even little happenings during the time of the trips and excavations. Christie seems to have written this travel memoir by means of recallings and remembrances. She remembered every detail no matter how tiny it was, which is an indication of her having a wide perspective to express every detail. Therefore, Christie's book also serves the assumption that Christie wrote the book by means of her noteworthy observations and noteworthy memory. As stated in a previous part of this study, it is known that Christie wrote *Come, Tell Me How You Live* by benefiting from her own diary. Osborne, like Campbell, has the idea that the book is "based upon journals which she had kept assiduously during her archaeological expeditions to the Middle East with Mallowan" (256). However, even if all these details existing in the book are accepted to be included in her diary, it is Christie who wrote everything in her diary in a realistic manner. If Christie had not had a sharp memory, she could not have reflected every incident, every person, their travels and excavations through vivid descriptions in *Come, Tell Me How You Live*.

Christie's work shows the reader the traveller's consciousness both before and during the travel. We see her consciousness both in the act of travel and also in the act of retrospection. Thus the book presents the reader with the moments when people they met and the journey, expeditions, excursions are being recalled and recounted.

The detailed descriptions of people in the book can be elaborated on through Mac's and Guilford's descriptions from Christie's own perspective: Mac is described as a young shy man having "coldly superior manner [...] gently raised eyebrows" and an "air of polite attention to words" (33). Guilford, the architect is introduced to the reader through not only physical qualities but also one of his deeds: "Guilford has a long, fair, serious face, and was once, at the beginning of his first season, very particular about the careful sterilizing and application of dressings to the local cuts and wounds (186).

Among numerous detailed desriptions of places in the book, two are suffice. The first one is the description of the environment of the hotel that the Mallowans stayed in Beyrout:

> BEYROUT! Blue sea, a curving bay, a long coastline of hazy blue mountains. Such is the view from the terrace of the Hotel. From my bedroom, which looks inland, I see a garden of scarlet poinsettias. The room is high, white, slightly prison-like in aspect. A modern wash-basin complete with taps and waste-pipe strikes a dashing modern note (32).

And the second is that of the bank where the Mallowans were present for their financial affairs:

> The Bank is of stone — large, cool, empty, very peaceful. There is a bench in the middle, on which sit two soldiers, an old man in picturesque

> coloured rags with a hennaed beard, and a boy in torn European clothing. They all sit peacefully gazing into space and occasionally spitting. There is a mysterious bed with dingy blankets in a corner. We are received with pleasure by the clerk behind the counter (118).

Likewise, incidents and situations are also given through vivid descriptions. For example, the ritual of drinking coffee is described in so realistic a manner that the reader has a mental picture of the situation:

> After courteous greetings, the great ones (ourselves, the foremen, Alawi and Yahya, the Sheikh and his chief friends) all sit down in a circle. An old man, handsomely apparelled, approaches us, bearing a coffee-pot and three little cups. A tiny drop of intensely black coffee is poured into each. The first one is handed to *me* – proof that the Sheikh is acquainted with the (extraordinary!) European custom of serving women first. Max and the Sheikh have the next two. We sit and sip. In due course another tiny drop is poured into our cups and we continue to sip. Then the cups are taken back, refilled, and Guilford and the foremen drink in their turn. So it goes on round the circle. A little distance away stands a considerable crowd of those of the second rank. From behind the partition of the tent close beside me come muffled giggles and rustlings. The Sheikh's womenfolk are peeping and listening to what goes on (187-188).

Despite all these details, Christie is observed to have said the things in a concise manner. This may be due to her "particular skill in the distilled short literary form" (Forshaw 22). This is a quality attributed to Christie as a writer of crime fiction by Barry Forshaw. It should be noted that Christie employed a realistic style in *Come, Tell Me How You Live*; however, she describes the events briefly and succinctly, which is a significant aspect especially in short fiction.

III. 2. Christie's creating the comic in the book:

Comedy is not a feature encountered in travel writings unless really funny events are told. Christie creates, in her book, comic scenes, some of which depend on really comic incidents and some of which are reflected as comic although they are not comic. The latter case is achieved by Christie through her own attitude towards the events. There are so many comic events that are told throughout the book to exemplify the first case. For instance, there are quite funny scenes in the first part of the book, where Christie explains how they prepared for the travel to Syria. The scene in which Christie says that her husband called her to sit on his suitcases because he could not close it after packing it arises smile in the reader's face even if it does not arise laughter. Christie writes:

> At nine a.m. I am called in as the heavy-weight to sit on Max's bulging suitcases.
>
> 'If you can't make them shut,' says Max ungallantly, 'nobody can!'
>
> The superhuman feat is finally accomplished by the aid of sheer avoirdupois, (25).

Throughout the book there are also instances in which one sees Christie's approach the things in a comical way. For example, when she gives an account of the shopping before the travel, she narrates the events in a comic style:

> But — yes — there are other things. Here is suitable wear for the wives of Empire Builders. Shantung! Plainly cut shantung coats and skirts — no girlish nonsense here — bulk is accommodated as well as scragginess! I depart into a cubicle with various styles and sizes. A few minutes later I am transformed into a memsahib! (20).

It is clear that Christie makes fun of her outward appearance when she wears the clothes which are suitable to the climate in the Middle East and would be convenient for both the travels and excavations there but do not reflect her dressing style. Christie's giving instructions to the salesperson when ordering hats with not so large brims (20-21), what she says about the travel suitcases with zips (25), and when her husband's comments on the flower patterns on her dress (24) are all given in a funny way.

Along with the aforementioned scenes, there are numerous comic scenes in the book including, for example, the incident of bug powder (Turkish Custom officials do not permit Christie to pass the border because they think she is carrying drug with her) (29), the scenes where they think the smell of the cheese forgotten in the cupboard is the smell of a dead mouse (124) and the Sheik's bringing his wives to Christie to relieve their headaches and cure other ailments (128). And upon this Christie's having a reputation for her "medical wisdom" (134) and other Arab and Kurdish women's coming to her to have cure and their having communication through pantomime-like movements because they do not know each other's language is equally comic. The Sheikh's thought that the bicarbonate, — which he calls "the white powder" — , which Christie has given him for his indigestion, has increased the Sheikh's sexual power and therefore he has now "two strong sons — twins" (135) is one of the funniest scenes in the book.

It would be better to conclude this section briefly with Max Mallowan's commentary on *Come, Tell Me How You Live* in his *Memoirs*, bringing out the humorous side of the book: "Agatha's gift for narrative, and for relating humorous exchanges of conversation between all manner of men and women in unusual situations, is rewardingly displayed" (Mallowan 205).

III. 3. Christie's creating curiosity in the book:

As we read *Come, Tell Me How You Live*, we, as readers, wonder if the archaeological team has found anything of archaeological and historical significance as a result of their excavations at the sites or tells of archaeological importance such as Habur, Jaghjagha, Chagar Bazar, Brak and etc. Instead of telling what the finds are as a result of the excavations and workings, Christie makes the reader wonder about this issue. This may be related to her attitude as a writer of detective fiction. In her detective stories, Christie does not solve the mystery till the end in order to maintain suspense and the reader's interest and wonder. While the story is proceeding, the reader is left in curiosity. Only at the end of the novel, the murderer is found and thus the mystery is solved. The case is not always but sometimes similar in *Come, tell Me How You Live* though the subject matter in it is not related to a crime or a murder, and though there is no mystery in it in the traditional sense. Instead of telling of the findings right away, Christie either focuses on other things or gives the information about finds connecting them to daily doings, comic eventsor conversations between people. And this arises curiosity in the reader. For this reason, as an author of detective fiction, Christie seems to have adopted a similar attitude toward her subject as an author of a travel memoir concerning archeological diggings, i.e. of *Come, Tell Me How You Live*. To elaborate on this idea, Christie's not mentioning the finds too much may be mentioned on page 124. It is known that, as stated by Campbell "in autumn 1936 the expedition dug up seventy cuneiform tablets which linked Chagar Bazar with the Royal House of Assyria – a significant historical find" (2005: 17). Despite the importance of finds, Christie glosses over them by saying "the first work period of ten days is just concluded, wit the bumper result of a find of nearly a hundred tablets, so everyone is jubilant" (124). Her giving informaton about the archeological diggings together with the events and conversations between people is observed in the parts in a scene where we are told that when their men dig a mound with fifteen layers to reach the virgin soil. Christie gives useful information about digging in a paragraph but finishes it with a mention of men's making joke to each other. Christie writes: "Of these [layers] the lower ten are prehistoric. After 1500 B.C. the mound was abandoned, presumably because denudation had set in and the levels were no longer good. There are, as always, some Roman and Islamic graves which are purely intrusive [...] but the men themselves are an irreverent lot. 'It is your grandfather we are digging up, Abdul!' 'No, it is yours, Daoud!' They laugh and joke freely" (146). It is obvious that Christie did not want to bore her readers by filling the book with too much archaeological information and created a fictional atmosphere in her book by focusing more on daily affairs and the relationships and conversations between people. Yet, one can find important facts about excavations, explorations, finds and works on those finds even if these are given together with the reflection of daily doings bulking large in the book.

The reflection of a really mysterious event is one of the elements that makes *Come, Tell Me How You Live* interesting for the reader. The scene is worth mentioning in the sense that it creates the tone of mystery in the book even if for a couple of seconds. During the excavations, Max's team found "many interesting carved animal amulets" that are typical but suddenly they begin to encounter some very curious blackened figures such as a bear, a lion's head and a primitive human figure. Upon this Max has suspicions and understands that they have been produced by a forger among them. As the workmen are given bakshish for each piece they find, somebody is thought to have probably produced them for money. Christie gives a brief summary of the investigation of this situation in the following sentences: "Detective work proceeds. The objects turn up in one corner of the dig and are usually found by one or other of two brothers" (146). In the follwing part of the scene we are informed that these men are exposed for fraud and they are fired. The situation is a micro sample of the uncovering of mystery in Christie's detective stories.

As a conclusion, it can be said that the creation and the solution of the mystery have been used by Agatha Christie in her travel memoir, which makes the book have a fiction-like quality.

III. 4. Christie's self-fashioning style in the book:

In *Come, Tell Me How You Live*, Christie does not only imply, by means of various ways, that the book was written by a professional author but also reflects her own identity as an author explicitly. This is particularly important because the reader, who is accustomed to reading Christie's detective novels, is likely to be in anticipation that he could find some qualities of her detective fiction in the book in his hand even though he knows it is a memoir. In other words, the reader is reminded of the author and thus the literariness of the book has become the subject of inquiry for the reader. To return to the scenes in which the author's identity is revealed, in a scene, we are told that Christie and her husband are talking about Mac, whom they were newly introduced, and are discussing what sort of a man he is. Then Christie questions whether Mac's silence is due to his shyness or his fear of Christie as her husband presumes. Mr. Mallowan tells her that Mac is "probably terrified of" her probably because she is a famous author. In the following excerpt, Christie is seen in a mental process in which she puts herself forward as an author:

> First of all, I say to myself, you are old enough to be Mac's mother. You are also an authoress — a well-known authoress. Why, one of your characters has even been the clue in a Times crossword. (High-water mark of fame!) And what is more, you are the wife of the Leader of the Expedition! Come now, if anyone is to snub anyone, it is you who will snub the young man, not the young man who will snub you (34)

There is a direct reference to her being an author on page 26. While saying goodbye to his relatives at Victoria Station, the author gives some admonishes to her sister. Among them, there is to contact with the publishers:

> write appropriately to the clergy-man who has discovered forty-three grammatical errors in my last book, and go through the seed-list for the garden and cross off vegetable marrows and parsnips? Yes, she will do all those things, and if any crisis occurs in the Home or the Literary World she will cable me. It doesn't matter, I say. She has a power of attorney. She can do anything she likes. She looks rather alarmed and says she shall be most careful (26).

Another direct reference to Christie's authorship is found when the Sheikh infers that Christie is a learned woman. Noting that she is "engaged on *The Times* crossword puzzzle, the Sheikh asks Christie's husband, Max, "so your Khatun reads? Does she also write?" Then we are told that "Max says that such is the case. 'A very learned Khatun ,' says the Sheikh appreciatively" (127-128).

As a conclusion, in *Come, Tell Me How You Live,* there are some scenes in which Christie reveals that the book was written by an author by means of the direct references to her authorship; and this drives one to think that one is reading a work of fiction due to the fact that Christie's reputation as a fiction writer is much more impressive than her authorship in her autobiographical writings. Therefore, it would not be wrong to conclude that Christie wrote *Come, Tell Me How You Live* by reflecting her own author identity to highlight the fictionality of the book.

IV. Agatha Christie's Use of the Languge in *Come, Tell Me How You Live*

The first thing the reader notices about the language used in *Come, Tell Me How You Live* is the use of a simple and plain English. Christie seems to have used the daily language. Another remarkable thing in the language is that Christie used many French and some Arabic expressions. In order not to distort the reality of the situations in which people spoke in French and Arabic, Christie gives them in their original form rather than translating them. To name a few, when Christie tells us that they are paid a visit by a French colleague and his architect, she reflects his speech in French: "After a pleasant visit they go off again. We admire their car. M. Parrot says sadly: *'Oui, c'est une bonne machine, mais elle va trap vite. Beaucoup trop vite.'* He adds: *'L'année dernière elle a tué deux de mes architectes!'* " (132). In another scene Arab workers' gratitude to God for their situation is given in their own language. Christie writes:

> On our way back to Chagar we meet large quantities of our workmen walking across country to the new dig.
>
> *'El hamdu lillah!'* they cry. 'Will there be work for us tomorrow?'
>
> 'Yes, there will be work.' (148).

The use of French and Arabic is an outcome of the conveyance of the speech of the speakers as they were. Besides, Christie sometimes uses French and Arabic words and expressions in her own sentences. To name a few, in one scene in the book, we are told that Madame Dunand's sentence is repeated to Mac, whose French is no more than saying "Qui" and "Non". Although the sentence is originally told by French lady, it is repeated by Christie: "*'Ah, votre petit architecte, il ne sait pas parler? Il a tout de même l'air intelligent!'* "(175). In the epiloge Christie expresses her wish of going to those places again by using an Arabic word meaning 'I hope'. This is also the last sentence of the book: "Inshallah, I shall go there again, and the things that I love shall not have perished from this earth. ...". And the book ends with a praise to God in Arabic: "El Hamdu Lillah" (205). Christie's use of French and communicating in French with people who cannot speak in English is a sign of Christie's being a learned woman. Her use of Arabic in her own sentences may be an indication of Christie's finding Arabic an exotic language.

Another important feature noticed in the book is the use of a literary language. In other words, Christie created ironies, simple similes and metaphors in her narrative. These figures of speech make the book enjoyable for the reader.

Furthermore, the rhetoric of the book has saved it from being direct and informative; and thus the book has become one close to fiction.

IV. 1. Ironic language in the book:

Christie created some ironies in *Come, Tell Me How You Live.* It is observed that Christie created them with an ease and they function as a means of entertainment in the book. To give an example to ironies, Christie, while ordering hats, is supposed to choose the colour of hats. She expresses this memory in these words: Victory! We select the colour — one of those new shades with the pretty names: Dirt, Rust, Mud, Pavement, Dust, etc." (Christie Mallowan, 1999: 21). It is obvious that on one hand, the author calls the names of the colours "pretty" but on the other hand the names include the names of the dirty things and places.

While mentioning cigarette smuggling, Christie calls this act of Easterners living in villages "an exact science", which is an ironic and humorous expression. In the explanation part, it is understood that the villagers actually do nothing to hide the cigarettes but take advantage the customs officers deficit. The part is in the following:

> The smuggling of cigarettes over the Iraq border appears to be almost an exact science. The Customs' car arrives at a village one day — and on the next the smugglers.... Max asks if the Customs never turn back and visit a village a second time. The man looks reproachful, and says of course not. If they did, everything would go wrong. As it is, the workmen happily smoke cigarettes that have cost them twopence a hundred! (133).

By means of this irony, Christie makes fun of the poor functioning of the Customs Office.

The use of ironies and ironical expressions proves in general that Christie benefited from her writing skills as an author and specifically that she used her gift of story-telling in a humorous way during the writing of *Come, Tell Me How You Live.*

IV. 2. Similes, metaphors and other comparisons, and the symbolic uses in the book:

Though the genre of *Come, Tell Me How You Live* does not belong to imaginative literature, it contains a number of figures of speech such as simile, metaphor, personification and symbol. The employment of all these figures of speech makes the book seem to be a fictional work.

Throughout her book, Christie makes resemblances between the things, people and situations. For example, a simile appears in the scene where the dresses in the store are resembled to "blooms of strange tropical flowers" due to their colours (26). She makes a resemblance between French architect (a friend of their French colleague's) and "an inferior saint" in respects of appearance and manner. She tells us that French architect "has one of those weak nondescript beards" and "says nothing but *'Merci, Madame,'* in polite negatives when offered anything" (132).

Christie's likening Abdullah's expression with that of a camel (62), her reflecting Hamoudie like "the serpent in Eden" when he wishes to earn extra money (69), her use of the image of "death" in order to express the extremity of her headache (46), Palmyra's enchanting beauty's having a dream-like quality (39), Yahya's likeness to "a friendly dog" (84) and B.'s "roaming around like a lost soul" (105) are some of the similes among many in the book. One of the original similes in the book appears when Christie tells us that "Women, children, hens, cats, dogs — all weeping, wailing, screaming, shouting, abusing, praying, laughing, miaowing, clucking and barking — depart slowly from the courtyard like some fantastic finale in an opera!" (79). Christie creates another simile highlighting the similarities between the behaviours, "singing and shaking a large whip" and the look of a drunkard Circassian having "high boots and gay wrappings" and the Russian ballet (132). In order to express her tiredness due to developing photographs in the dark room, Christie creates a simile: "I emerge from my dark-room feeling exactly like a bit of wall fungus myself" (154).

The reference to gambling to define archeological diggings is a metaphor that was created by Christie. In order to state the idea of uncertainty and of risk, she writes: "All digging is a gamble" (59). Another similarity was constructed in the form of metaphor in the scene where Christie and her husband remember their dog Swiss Miss when they learn that Ali has gone to Kamichlie and come back by bike, that is, he has travelled fifty miles on a bicycle, and additionally "bicycled to the village of Germayir, eight kilometres away" to see a friend of his. They make a similarity between Ali and their dog Swiss Miss because he has traveled such a long distance in a short time with no sign of fatigue. The likeness between Ali and their dog Swiss Miss appears in this sentence: "My solicitude on Ali's behalf is abruptly damped, especially when he assists with waiting at table at dinner-time with a radiant face and no signs of fatigue" (130). We are told that the Mallowans had Swiss Miss in Mosul and she broke a leg and became cripple. Despite her limping, after two years when the Mallowans went to Mosul again, they saw Swiss Miss there, having a family now. This is the indication of her resistance against hardships for the Mallowans, who expected her to die during their absence. Christie ends the dog's story saying that "[s]ince then, when I start indulging in anxieties, the words Swiss Miss are used to quell my objections!" (130) to imply the idea that when she is anxious about Ali, she is reminded of Swiss Miss by Max. Recalling her wife Swiss Miss, Max soothes her and she is persuaded that everything will be alright.

Come, Tell Me How You Live contains some symbols along with similes and metaphors. An original symbol appears in the first chapter. Christie defines Victoria Station as the "gateway to the world beyond England" (25). Another symbol in the book is the Eastern world itself. For most of the Europeans, the East is an exotic, mysterious, enchanting and romantic world. The case is not different for Christie. Christie, from time to time in her book, reflects the Eastern world as impressive and fascinating. For instance, when they leave Beyrout by boat, the scenery is reflected as glamorous and romantic. Christie writes: "How lovely it is, this coast with the mountains of the Lebanon standing up dim and blue against the sky! There is nothing to mar the romance of the scene. One feels poetical, almost sentimental. ..." (203).

She describes the train they got on at Victoria Station to go to İstanbul as "a big snorting, hurrying, companionable train"(25). The description of the train contains a figure of speech — personification, which shows that Christie could not prevent herself creating such images containing figures of speech although she seemed to be writing an informative text.

During a travel to Tell Hamidi, to start the machine of the car and move it Hamoudi gives instructions to Aristide. In the reflection of this scene, Christie attributes two adjectives to the car though these adjectives were not used by Hamouidi. Thus Christie created personification in the relevant expression: "Not so, he [Hamoudi] seems to say, should you treat a high-mettled and nervous car!" (58). It is clear that the attribution of two human qualities 'being high-mettled" and 'being nervous' to an inanimate object — car is personification.

Christie creates an enjoyable personification when she gives an account of the cat, which was taken there with the duty of catching mice in the house:

> Our cat arrives at dinner-time. I shall never forget that cat! It is [...] a highly professional cat. It knows the job for which it has been engaged, and proceeds to get on with it in a truly specialized manner.
>
> Whilst we dine, it crouches in ambush behind a packing-case. When we talk, or move, or make too much noise, it gives us an impatient look.

> 'I must request of you,' the look says, 'to be quiet. How can I get on with the job without co-operation?'
>
> So fierce is the cat's expression that we obey at once, speak in whispers, and eat with as little clinking of plates and glasses as possible (81).

Christie's creation of a cat as a speaking figure through its look is enjoyable.

It is obvious that all these figures of speech were employed in *Come, Tell Me How You Live* through Christie's gift of writing and that they all contribute to the literariness of the book and thus make the book a pleasure to read.

V. Thematic Aspects of Come, Tell Me How You Live

Theme is a significant element of fiction and it stands for the main ideas conveyed by means of the stories in novels, short stories, dramatic works and poems. Theme is the universal idea that is inferred from the work. The employment of themes is a quality that the genres in imaginative literature are supposed to have. Though *Come; Tell Me How You Live* is a work of non-fiction, it seems to employ in itself some themes, which are stated indirectly. There are actually two significant central ideas that can be apprehended by inference in Christie's travel memoir. One of them is the cultural interaction between the western and the eastern culture. It seems to be a recurrent theme in the book. The other is memory, which is reflected as a reliable means of reflecting the truths. The following two parts of the study aim to explain and analyze briefly the employment of these central ideas in *Come, Tell Me How You Live*.

V. 1. The reflection of the cultural interactions in the book:

Those who read Christie's *Come, Tell Me How You Live* notice that the book reveals themes in it as a work of fiction does. This is one important aspect of fiction, which is related with the intention of the author. As we all know, a literary work contains important ideas in itself and the author reveals these major ideas by means of the story he has created. One interesting theme in *Come, Tell Me How You Live* is the encounter between the westerners and easterners. Related to this, some other themes such as cultural interactions and the reflection of the East and eastern people from the perspective of the westerner arise in the book. As mentioned earlier in the study, the book is crowded with many peoople from different nationalities. Throughout the book, cultural differences between these people arise in many scenes due to their different ways of life and different traditions. In order to illustrate them, some scenes from the book may be cited. For instance, the belligerent nature of the Arabs is reflected in the book as their general trait in their personality and also a trait taking part in their way of life. Christie writes: "A violent quarrel breaks out after the work between the hot-tempered Alawi and Serkis, our carpenter. It arises, as usual, out of nothing at all, but reaches murderous heights" (129). In another scene we are told that Ferhid and Ali "never stop quarrelling" (139). Arabs' quarrelsome nature is reflected in the following expressions as well: "Various minor complications occur. Four men are sacked for persistent fighting. Alawi and Yahya have a quarrel and will not speak to each other" (157). The book has many scenes similar to the scenes cited above. It is obvious that Christie observed that Arabs frequently quarrel with each other, sometimes for nothing even if the problem could have been solved by means of communication. This is a reflection of the differences between the eastern and western cultures. Along with their quarrelsome nature, Arabs' humorous side is another trait that Christie reflects in her book by means of numberless examples.

Christie observed many different traditions of the eastern people and depicted them in her book as the qualities characterizing the eastern people. For example, the Sheikhs's having many wives is frequently referred to in the book (128, 134-136). Likewise, other Arabs such as Hamoudi, who is told to have wives (69) and a watchman having three wives (138) are referred to as men following the tradition of polygamy.

Cultural differences are experienced between the people on the level of language as well. In effect, the area where cultural difference emerges most clearly is the area of language. There are many scenes in the book to exemplify the case. To name one example, we can give the scene where Christie was misunderstood by the Turkish Customs officials, who thought that Christie was carrying drug with herself, seeing a bottle of bug powder in her suitcase. Due to the fact that Christie did not understand them and they did not understand Christie, there arose a lack of communication, which has been reflected in a comic way in the book. Language becomes a barrier again in another scene in which Christie and Ebu Suleiman's wife have to have communication through pantomime-like movements. Here Christie, like a doctor, advices the woman to bath her eyes with the liquid she gives. This comic scene, too, reveals the cultural difference:

> Final pantomime of the bathing of eyes.
>
> The patient then responds by a pantomime of drinking a copious draught. I shake my head. *Outward* application — to the *eyes*. The patient is a little

> disappointed. However, we hear next day [...] She bathed her eyes with it, and then drank it all, every drop! (134)

Sometimes a reverse situation occurs despite the different nationalities of people. We see that communication is sustained between Christie and other European people because Christie could speak French. As an example, we can take the scene in which Christie, her husband and M. le Director speak in French on highly serious matters such as politics (119). This is a reflection of the cultural affinity.

In connection with the above themes, it may be argued that *Come, Tell Me How You Live* was constructed according to the western understanding of the time: the westerner is always reflected as the one who goes to distant places to explore, goes on journeys, who searches for and finds new things. On the other hand, the east and the easterner are reflected as the object of research, searched by the westerner. Correspondingly, the book seems to support the assumption that only the West has produced noteworthy travellers, researchers and scientists. Here, we can say that Agatha Christie adopted the orientalist attitude towards the east and eastern people, which we revealed in our previous studies dealing with Christie's two novels having orientalist settings, *Death On the Nile* and *Appointment with Death.* The studies approach these novels from the perspective of Postcolonial Criticism inaugurated by Edward Said with his groundbreaking work *Orientalism* and offer detailed analyses of the delineation of the Orient and oriental in Christie's novels (Zengin 1; Zengin 2).

Independent of the aforementioned themes, determination and grit of man in front of hard work, the place of such human values as benevolence, hospitality and kindness in human's life, human's ability to withstand difficulties, human's relations in general, man's interaction with nature and natural elements such as animals, and etc. are among the main ideas that emerge in *Come, Tell Me How You Live*. Since how all these themes are revealed in the book will be extensive enough to be the subject of another study, we will put them aside now. Instead, we will suffice to say that although *Come, Tell Me How You Live* is a travel memoir, various themes emerge in it behind the various stories constructed skillfully by Christie.

V. 2. Memory as a reliable means of reflecting the truth:

No memory is dim for Christie in *Come, Tell Me How You Live*. Christie seems to have been able to recall and reflect many events and incidents in her book. Concentrating on incidents and people, Christie also seems to have remembered all those people she had met during both her travels and her life in Syria. This is partly because Christie was a careful observer and an analyst of the situations having even subtle details and partly because she followed common practice of carrying and writing a diary during that time and then she made use of it during the writing of *Come, Tell Me How You Live*. Campbell states that "Christie began a diary that formed the basis of her memoir *Come,Tell Me How You Live*" at Chagar Bazar in Syria (Campbell 17). Christie herself wrote, in the "Epilogue" of the book, that she had written some "notes and rough diaries" (205) during those years spent in the Middle East. Yet, it may be reckoned that Christie must have made use of her sharp memory and her wide perspective to express everything in detail in the book if we consider that everything she wrote in *Come, Tell Me How You Live* had not been written in her diary.

In respect of the reflection of the memorable events, *Come, Tell Me How You Live* offers the reader two different kinds of memories. The first one includes the memories gained by Christie during the travels, explorations, excavations and their life in Syria in general. The latter contains the memories gained by Christie in a previous time, namely, during the time before the time that is reflected in the book. Although these do not take place much in the book, they show not only that the author wrote these memories in detail via her sharp memory but also that the book has a form of memory within memory. For instance the memory about Swiss Miss is not a distant memory for Christie. She recalls the crippled dog's story in detail when she worries about Ali, who travels a very long way by bike, yet shows no sign of tiredness (130). As Swiss Miss's story has already been given briefly in a previous part, the details of the story would not be given here. What matters about this story is that in *Come, Tell Me How You Live* Christie does not only transmit her memories in the actual time of the memory but also remembers and gives a past memory of hers in it. Therefore, it can be said Christie gives memory within memory in the book.

Conclusion

Agatha Christie was already a well-known author of detective fiction when she wrote and published her only travel memoir *Come, Tell Me How You Live: An Archeological Memoir* which is a realistic yet charming account of the Mallowans' adventures during the archeological diggings in Syria and the area known as Mesopotamia in Iraq between the years 1935 and 1938. Throughout this study, *Come, Tell Me How You Live* has been analyzed to indicate that Christie wrote this book wrote this book with an awareness that she was an author par excellence and by the employment of either direct references to or indirect implications of her authorship. The study has revealed that on the one hand Christie reflects her authorship through some direct sentences, expressions or situations in the text, but on the other hand, she implies her authorship during the creation of her book by means of the employment of the elements of fiction although the book is a travel memoir — a genre belonging to the non-imaginative literature. Namely, she wrote this book in a way that implies the idea that the author of the book is not an occasional writer; rather, she is a fiction writer. Therefore, *Come, Tell Me How You Live*, though based on real life experiences and travel memories of the author, presents the reader with a pleasure of reading because it arises a feeling in the reader that it is not only an informative travel account or a tasteless memoir but an enjoyable book containing many memories, written through the employment of elements of fiction, expressed in a literary language and in both a realistic and humorous style. Correspondingly, it has been argued that the book can be defined as an auto fictional text, during the reading of which, the reader has a pleasure of reading fiction.

The study focuses on the ways or devices that Christie employed to create a fiction-like work. She has been observed that she benefited from such elements of fiction as plot, characterization, narrative methods, style, the figurative language, tone and theme in the construction of the book. In separate parts, the author's use of such devices in her book has been analyzed by means of the references to the relevant scenes.

As a conclusion, Christie's use of self-consciousness seems to highlight the literariness and fictionality of *Come, Tell Me How You Live*, which presents the reader an experience of a pleasurable reading of a travel memoir which was written as a reminiscent of Christie's experiences and life with her husband, Max Mallowan, who was an archeologist, in the Middle East during the time before World War II.

Bibliography

Campbell, Mark. *Agatha Christie*. Great Britain: Cox & Wyman, Reading, 2005.

Carroll, Lewis. *The Complete Works of Lewis Carroll* (Intr. Alexander Woollcott, illustr. John Tenniel). NewYork: Vintage Books, 1976.

Christie, Agatha. *Agatha Christie: An Autobiography.* United Kingdom: Harper Collins, Inc., 2010.

Forshaw, Barry. *The Rough Guide to Crime Fiction.* London: Penguin Books Ltd., 2007.

Mallowan Christie, Agatha. *Come, Tell Me How You Live: An Archeological Memoir*. (intr. Jacquetta Hawkes). United Kingdom: Harper Collins, Inc., 1999.

Mallowan, Max E. L. (1977). *Mallowan's Memoirs.* New York : Dodd, Mead. Accessed from https://archive.org/details/mallowansmemoirs00mall/page/n11/mode/2up on 01.10.2022

Osborne, Charles. *The Life and Crimes of Agatha Christie*. London: HarpersCollins Publishers, 1999.

Zengin, Mevlüde. "Western Image Of The Orient And Oriental In Agatha Christie's *Death On The Nile*: A Postcolonial Reading". *Gaziantep University Journal of Social Sciences*, vol. 15, no. 3, 2016(1), pp. 837-866.

Zengin, Mevlüde. "Orientalism in Agatha Christie's Appointment with Death". *ASOS Journal: The Journal of Academic Social Science.* vol. 4, no. 32, 2016(2), pp. 99-114.

A Short Bio of Assoc. Prof. Dr. Mevlüde ZENGİN

Mevlüde ZENGİN received her PhD at Ankara University, Faculty of Languages and History-Geography, Department of English Language and Literature in 2007. She is currently an Assoc. Prof. of English Language and Literature at Sivas Cumhuriyet University, Faculty of Letters. Her main research interests include the modernist novel in English Literature and novel, poetry, short story as literary genres, literary theory and criticism, and New Historicism. She is the writer of various essays published in both national and international journals and book chapters on English literature.

Bartolomé de Las Casas' Travel Writing: *A Short Account of the Destruction of the Indies* in the Light of Renaissance Humanism

Assoc. Prof. Dr. Gül KOÇSOY

Abstract

A Spanish bishop and missionary **Bartolomé de Las Casas** (1484-1566) wrote *A Short Account of the Destruction of the Indies* (1552) to tell the atrocities done by the Spaniards to the indigenous people, Natives in the first decades of the Spanish colonization of the West Indies. Although he is a clergyman, he gives priority to humanist concerns. He renders different places, cultures and languages. His work is ideological in that he documents slavery, defends the rights of them, tells the situation to King Charles I of Spain and urges the pope to end the persecutions. Against harsh exploitation and colonization, he offers a milder and more humane colonization. As a Renaissance humanist, he cherishes the importance of education and the promotion of universal virtues, realizing individuals' potential both for their own good and for the improvement of society. He prescribes the education of the natives for an easier and justifiable colonization. Following Humanist ethics, he is respectful to the natives' culture. He questions the meaning of Christianity and humanity. The work is used by English colonizers to discredit the Spanish rule and Catholicism. It was banned in Spain for some time. Las Casas has achieved some legal improvement of the natives and leaves a heritage of humanist and humanitarian perspective to the Native American people. He proves that the idea that the indigenous people are less than human is completely wrong and unjust.

Keywords: Renaissance Humanism, Travel Writing, Missionary, English colonizers, Indigenous people.

Introduction

The Renaissance (1485-1660) which began in Italy is characterized by skepticism towards the church and other established social institutions. "The Renaissance (from the French word for 'rebirth') refers to the emergence and new interest in classical Greek and Roman texts and culture that took place between the Middle Ages and the modern period" (Milne 682). On the other hand, the word 'humanism' enters the philosophy vocabulary in the 19th century with the philosophers who see the ancient Greek culture as the core and root of the western civilization and the Renaissance (1485-1660) as the extension of it. Humanism is a cultural movement that began in the Renaissance when the Renaissance scholars read the ancient literature. Humanists studied humanities (liberal arts) grammar, history, poetry, and philosophy. They tried to form a link between the ancient thought and Christianity, being respectful to Christian ideology. Instead of religion, a scientific, critical, rational and progressive attitude toward life is adopted in cultural, historical and social scene. For human nature is competent, reverence and reliance on man is essential. Human autonomy of consciousness, virtue and morality is important for them.

"In modern times, the term 'humanism' has gained a different meaning (a rational and non-religious way of life) and so to safeguard its original purpose, when applied to 1400-1600, it is often clarified as 'Renaissance Humanism'" ('Renaissance Humanism' *World History Encyclopedia* 2022). For the Renaissance humanists 'man is the measure of all things' [1] and he can/should decide his fate; he should not permit anything to decide his fate. Protagoras by this phrase means that man is the center of the universe instead of God, inspiring the Renaissance intellectuals and later the Romantics. Man should gain human honor through his own effort and mind power. Renaissance Humanism cherishes ancient and old Greek culture. It reacts against the scholastic Middle-Age mentality and religion based lifestyle. Despite being secular, the humanists were not against the Church. It is an ideal aiming at constituting an entity of philosophy, history, literature and philosophy of ethics (studia humanitatis). It also adopts secularism in education both in academic and personal development. Humanists cherish the importance of education and the promotion of universal virtues, realizing individuals' potential both for their own good and for the improvement of society. "Renaissance man, also called Universal Man,... that 'a man can do all things if he will.' The ideal embodied the basic tenets of

[1] This phrase belongs to the ancient Greek philosopher Protagoras (490BC?-420BC?) and it passes in Plato's work *Protagoras*.

Renaissance humanism, which considered man the centre of the universe, limitless in his capacities for development, and led to the notion that men should try to embrace all knowledge and develop their own capacities as fully as possible" ('Renaissance Man' *Britannica*). So, the ideal man for the humanists is the one who develops himself mentally, morally and physically, has diverse interests and studies, and believes human improvement as endless.

The Renaissance thinkers/humanists like Francesco Petrarch, Lorenzo Valla, Girolamo Savonarola, Pico della Mirandola, Desiderius Erasmus, Leonardo da Vinci, Michalengelo, Raphael, Thomas More, Copernicus, Galileo, Martin Luther, Miguel de Cervantes, Francis Bacon, Christopher Marlowe, Montaigne, François Rabelais and William Shakespeare aim at leading humanity to a better position but did not share their ideas on all subjects. Their common point is that they regard the virtuous individual as supreme and desire him to fully participate in proper social life. They see man as a dignified value and a self-sufficient, potent and privileged being attributing priority to him. He should exert efforts to produce unique.

In this context, the Renaissance travelers also aim at improving themselves and expand their knowledge of the world as well as indoctrinating the natives of the newly-found lands with Christian belief and catechism, for the Renaissance is an age of colonial and ideological exploration. The interest in both the old and new knowledge leads Renaissance intellectuals to see new places or universities in the world. Since the aim of travel writing is to state the different manners, cultures and languages in a place, as well as to describe the place with its general or detailed elements and geographical historical, sociological and aspects, the Renaissance travelers crave for learning about these issues. "In Renaissance learning geography, or cosmography, acted as an encyclopaedic synthesis for the description of the world. Therefore, the description of peoples became the empirical foundation for a general rewriting of 'natural and moral history' within a new cosmography made possible by the navigations of the period" (Rubiés 242). The Renaissance travelers reflect their own experiences, reactions, feelings, thoughts, ideas and their experience of the cultural encounters in text and image forms. The good-intentioned travelers make dangerous journeys facing with bandits, thieves, pseudo-monks, vagabonds, various life-threatening vagrancy and abuse while visiting different places.

As a literary genre "travel writing consists of predominantly factual, first-person prose accounts of travels that have been undertaken by the author-narrator. It includes discussion of works that some may regard as genres in their own right, ... but it distinguishes these from other types of narrative in which travel is narrated by a third party or is imagined" (Youngs 3). The Renaissance travelers render their interaction and travel experience in the first person singular. In these factual accounts, they describe such issues as missionary work, piracy, captivity, identity, cultural difference, the superiority of Western civilization, education, archaeology, history, war and commerce through their own point of view. These writings tempt the readers to develop and adopt the new and different ideologies, interpretations and views. As the writers express their power in their narrative voices, they are able to influence public consciousness and awareness about many socio-economic, historical and moral spheres.

A Spanish bishop, missionary, historian and traveler Bartolomé de Las Casas (1474 or 1484? -1566) is not an exception to having an influential role on his readers' ideas. He is one of the first defenders of international human rights and receives a good education on religion and law. First, he goes to Hispaniola (West Indies) in 1502 which was discovered in 1492 and joins some scouting trips and military expeditions. He returns to Europe in 1506, is appointed as a high-ranking clergyman in Rome. In 1512, he becomes the first friar in the New World. He learns native languages. He introduces the natives as civilized who can make functional roads; they are hospitable, helpful and amicable, but physically fragile. They live like saints with minimum property. They are curious about Christianity and ready to be converted to Christianity. Their lands are fertile and full of underground mines with mild climate. Later, Las Casas goes to Spain in 1515, tells the persecutions committed upon the natives by the soldiers and sailors. In 1516 he again returns to America as a member of the commission investigating the atrocities done to the natives; for instance, some epidemics of diseases brought by the Europeans also decreases their population. In 1520, he criticizes the atrocities to the Spanish King Carlos V, who enacts a law forbidding slavery. In 1537, both the Spanish king and the pope determine to ban making the natives work as slaves and confiscate their goods and lands. Upon going to America in 1544, he sees again that the colonialists' main aim is to be rich, not religion or to explain Christianity. According to him, the wars and massacres are unjustifiable, because until they begin slaughtering, the natives do not attack or kill them. The Spanish colonists use unproportional force either by war or slavery. For him, it is a great sin to destroy natural assets, evacuate the lands and cancel kingdoms. He feels urged to tell all these phenomena there as a responsive Renaissance intellectual/traveler.

Las Casas writes a tract *A Short Account of the Destruction of the Indies* in 1552 to tell the abuse and atrocities done by the Spaniards to the indigenous people, Native Americans at the time of colonization. He at first does not carry any sensitivity about colonialism but later his conscience sees the terrible facts; he sees the unjustly treated natives, assaulted by the tyrant conquerors, and dedicates his life to their defense by peaceful means.

At first, he too holds some Indians in *encomienda*; "an encomienda (from Spanish *encomendar*, "to entrust") consisted of a grant by the crown to a conquistador, a soldier, an official, or others of a specified number of "Indios" (Native Americans and, later, Filipinos) living in a particular area. The receiver of the grant, the encomendero, could exact tribute from the "Indios" in gold, in kind, or in labour and was required to protect them and instruct them in the Christian faith" ('Encomienda' Encyclopedia Britannica). The Spaniards also control the natives' lands informally. They force them to work under heavy conditions for long periods with scarce nutrition. He abandons his encomienda life in 1515 because he sees the drawbacks and maltreatments in the system. He offers a milder encomienda, or abolition of it completely. He feels ethically responsible to relate the Europeans the cultural context of the lands. He feels himself in complicity if he does not explicate the hard conditions. His rhetoric shows clearly that he has received a vast education and knew ecclesiastical law. "Bartolomé de Las Casas, a Spanish cleric, Dominican friar, and New World bishop, is considered one of the major figures in the sixteenth- century critique of the conquest and colonization of the American hemisphere" (Orique 32). Just like the other clergymen, he attempts to preserve the natives from the brutality, lust, violence and greed of the Spanish colonizers. He makes trans-Atlantic journeys and goes to Germany to speak to the clergy and the Emperor there. Some authorized people including several prominent historians defend the wars against the natives, against their religion (idolatry), serfdom, exploitation of their lands and goods. It can sound terrible for the 21st century people, but in those times these injustices are generally regarded as normal by many people.

When Las Casas complains the situation to the King Ferdinand I, then to the Cardinal he arouses much animosity and reproach in the Spaniards. He states that the exploiters catch the Indians with mastiffs, butcher men, women and children alike, whip, box, beat and molest making them afraid of them. While behaving like that they aim at subduing them through fear; they do not employ friendly ways or get along well with them to settle there. He defends the idea that the natives can be converted to Christianity only through peaceful ways, be integrated to the Christian community and become civilized. Though different they can easily be converted to Christianity because they are submissive and good-natured people. With these ideas, Las Casas exhibits that he has the universal conception of man, a typical Renaissance thought. "Like other humanists, he was painfully aware of the shortcomings of Old-World Christianity and of European culture, and he sought to recover the unrealized glories of the Christian and secular pasts" (Orique 15). Christianization becomes difficult, because the Spaniards are not good character models. Las Casas eyewitnesses and condemns the depopulation, crimes, repartimiento (dividing the natives after conquest) evils and harms against the innocent by the officials including governors and other administrators. He stresses that the main aim of Spanish existence is to convert and evangelize the Indigenous peoples in peaceful ways, but unfortunately the ambition of gold, jewelry, sugar and other resources predominates this religious goal.

The Indians hate the Spaniards and Christianity; one of the chiefs remarks: "he said, they adore a certain Covetous Deity, whose cravings are not to be satisfied by a few moderate offerings, but they may answer his Adoration and Worship, demand many unreasonable things of us, and use their utmost endeavors to subjugate and afterwards murder us. Then taking up a Cask or Cabinet near at hand, full of Gold and Gems, he proceeded in this manner: This is the *Spaniards* God,…" (Las Casas 9) The Indians understand the real intention of the Spaniards, which is to exterminate all the natives, to learn the places of mineral deposits, and doom them to starvation by threat, torture, torment, infliction, grinding work, oppression, persecution, saevetia, travail, maltreatment, aggrievance, hardship, massacre, genocide, carnage, sabering, rampage, plunder, rape, devastation, tyranny, bullying, despotism, extortion, violence, pillage, burning alive, and many others. They dismantle Indian families by giving wives to sailors or soldiers and exchange thirty natives for a horse. They throw the fugitives from the cliffs. They sear them to signify slavery and if they rebel, they amputate their noses, ears or lips. Out of hunger, the natives have to eat other dead men. The Spaniards slander the king that he ordered them to subjugate, make slaves and kill them, which are unethical and unreal for the natives. Las Casas finds them sinful as a conscientious Renaissance priest and is glad that the commanders are punished severely by God; they die in terrible accidents as divine justice occurs.

Las Casas constantly warns other monks and complain about the inflictions, seeing them as inhumane. He reflects the conflict between the clergy and military forces. He inquires how under these unethical and deprecating conditions the natives can be converted to Christianity. He shares the native people's pain and the encomienda system and asks emotionally: "I desire therefore that the Readers who have or shall peruse these passages, would please seriously to consider whether or no, such Barbarous, Cruel and Inhumane Acts as these do not transcend and exceed all the impiety and tyrrany, which can enter into the thoughts or imagination of Man, and whether these *Spaniards* deserve not the name of Devils. For which of these two things is more eligible or desirable whether the *Indians* should be delivered up to the Devils themselves to be tormented or the *Spaniards*?" **(36)** This is an ethic question posed by a sensitive Renaissance thinker. It prescribes anger and hatred against the military forces, who have no sincere intention to teach the innocent natives the Bible in the New World. According to Las Casas, the military and royal forces hamper the clergymen's missionary activities because if the clergymen succeed in telling the real doctrines and catechism of Christianity, they will not get benefit from the riches easily and fast for the natives will not be willing to give their goods and properties. This proves that the military and royal forces still persist in exhibiting an unethical attitude. They compel the natives to accept Christianity by force and as a duty given by the king. Behaving like that, they make the natives become critical and cold to Christianity.

Moreover, the Spaniards forcibly usurp the natives' belongings. If they do not bring the amount of grain or gold they want or at the time they desire, they fetter them with irons, burden them with heavy sacs and force them to walk. Many of them die of starvation, thirst, and tiredness. They seize the extra grain they hid for the caution, starvation, drought or future generations. When famine appears, they die, of course. If they escape from the violence, they become preys to wild animals. The Spanish forces collect the orphans and one child from the family with two children. They make them slaves and send them to other places by ships. Many of them die of unaccustomed climate. On the other hand, Las Casas finds the natives noble: they determine to war instead of accepting slavery. According to him, they are very keen on their individual and national freedom and that means their ideas of freedom are consistent with the Renaissance humanism. The unproportional force and sharp swords of the Spanish defeat the primitive spears and arrows. The trained and rapacious Spanish army governors exacerbate the situation against the natives, killing their kings and *casics* by torture. They destroy the local languages and civilizations, the ancient cultures of the southern America; different objects of handicraft made of gold and silver are melted and taken to Spain. Upon seeing the injustices, Las Casas opposes them and gives up his Indian slaves, begins defending the rights of them and tells the real situation to King Charles I of Spain. Against harsh colonization, he offers a milder colonization, at least.

With the benignant behaviors of the monks, the natives gradually become Christians and build churches, but the soldiers in malice and depravement usurp their idols and require gold for giving them back. Thus, the natives question their Christianity. The monks beg the military forces to leave. The forces persuade the natives that the monks invited them. The natives try to kill the monks, seeing the monks as responsible for the wickedness. The Spanish forces oblige the natives to collect pearls under the sea for long durations and cause their deaths by sharks or they become sick by their lungs. It is clear that they are merciless and behave against God's order. When Germans come after the Spaniards, they are not different in terms of maltreatment and corruption. Las Casas is glad that several laws are enacted in 1542, forbidding the persecutions and sins. "It was not only with emotion and humanitarian ideals that Las Casas tried to alleviate the plight of the Indians, but also with the logic of the law" (Pennington, Jr. 161). As encomienda is "the official consignment of groups of Indians to privileged Spanish colonists who were entitled to receive tribute and labor from them,..." (Adorno 252) *encomenderos* and merchants in a short time become tyrants, robbers, killers and abusers. Las Casas is extremely against the encomienda system as well as the tyranny imposed by the Spanish. As he lives and works for missionary among them, he is able to save them from the violence of war, slavery and the encomienda to a great extent where he goes as a Renaissance traveler.

Las Casas defends the humanistic rights of the indigenous peoples tenaciously and in an altruistic way. He risks his own life and religious career while/for telling the persecutions. "Las Casas crossed the Atlantic no less than twelve times (what a horrible series of voyages in those days) to make interest for his Indians" (Wilkinson 45). The royal authority out of the great distance is not able to control the greedy colonizers and adventurers; moreover, clergymen have little impact on them. He struggles both with the colonizers, royal /military forces and the opposing clergymen. He is seen as a heretic by most of the monks, for "[t]he Spanish Churchmen were ever famous for their uncompromising morality" (Wilkinson 39). His anger against the colonists is for the basic human rights of the oppressed races. He reflects the plight of the Indians in his historical and theological piece of writing. "Only one edition of Las Casas' *Very Brief Account* appeared in Spain during the seventeenth century;..." (Keen 704) The work is used by English colonizers to discredit the Spanish rule and Catholicism and banned in Spain in 1659 completely. Las

Casas protests the iniquities like many other good-intentioned priests and aspires to amalgamate Biblical justice with humanistic ideals. He contends that the natives deserve respect and love like other peoples. He urges to observe an ethical stance in colonization. He claims the prevalent idea that the indigenous people are less than human is completely wrong and unjust. "He has come to be recognized as a political theorist of importance, and as one of the first anthropologists of America. Likewise his contributions in the fields of geography, philosophy, and theology are being studied today" (Hanke 29). While reflecting the first decades of the Spanish colonization of the West Indies, he epitomizes the cultural and historical context with local features.

Conclusion

In his own narrative authoritative voice Las Casas as a Renaissance humanist and traveler represents and develops new perspectives on the *new* world with shifting borders and the prerogatives of the newcomers. He is changed after his travel experience psychologically and ideologically. He begins challenging the ingrained ideas about the superiority of Western civilization. In the wars of religion, the struggles to Christianize the natives (in fact the real reason is to take possession of the riches), he urges the pope to end the persecutions, documents slavery, violence and the history and social conditions of the place. He questions the meaning of Christianity and humanity in his work and through it he achieves some legal improvement of the natives. In his *'exposé'* he blames, criticizes the cruel and abusive Spanish colonization through depicting violent images. He is respectful to the natives' culture in accordance with the humanist ethics and leaves a heritage of humanist and humanitarian perspective toward the native American people. "He placed its people unequivocally within the human family and the full plan of salvation history. He sought the universal application of justice and of law-divine, natural, and human. He sought the total well-being (eternal and temporal) of the Indigenous, as he advocated transnationally for needed change" (Orique 20) He deals with the issues of the discovery, conquest and gruesome colonization. He reports the ignominy and treachery of both the royal, military and clerical officials. His sensibilities as a reformer illustrate his moral judgment in the face of colonial abuse. "Finally, Las Casas's endeavors had a consistent international character as he persistently sought to influence royal and ecclesial authorities on both sides of the Atlantic" (Orique 7). He offers many common universal rules of conduct. Although he is a traveling clergyman, he gives priority to humanist concerns and sees all men equal as a Renaissance humanist.

Bibliography

Adorno, Rolena. "Discourses on Colonialism: Bernal Díaz, Las Casas, and the Twentieth-Century Reader". MLN, (March) Vol. 103 (2), Hispanic Issue. pp. 239-258 1988. https://www.jstor.org/stable/2905341 Accessed 21 July 2022.

"Encomienda". Encyclopedia Britannica. https://www.britannica.com/topic/encomienda Accessed 4 November 2022.

Hanke, Lewis. "Bartolomé De Las Casas and the Spanish Empire in America: Four Centuries of Misunderstanding" Proceedings of the American Philosophical Society. (February) Vol. 97, No. 1 pp. 26-30 American Philosophical Society 1953. https://www.jstor.org/stable/3143727 Accessed 21 July 2022.

Keen, Benjamin. "The Black Legend Revisited: Assumptions and Realities" The Hispanic American Historical Review. November Vol. 49(4). pp. 703-719 1969. https://www.jstor.org/stable/2511162 Accessed 27 July 2022.

Las Casas, Bartolome de. *A Brief Account of the Destruction of the Indies*. http://www.gutenberg.org/ebooks/20321 Accessed 25 July 2022.

"Renaissance Humanism". World History Encyclopedia. https://www.worldhistory.org/Renaissance_Humanism/#:~:text=Renaissance%20Humanism%20was%20an%20intellectual,out%20'lost'%20ancient%20manuscripts. Accessed 30 March 2022.

Milne, Ira Mark. *Literary Movements for Students*. New York: Gale Cengage Learning, 2009.

Orique, David T. "Journey to the Headwaters: Bartolomé de las Casas in a Comparative Context". The Catholic Historical Review (January) Vol. 95(1) pp. 1-24 2009. https://www.jstor.org/stable/27745441 Accessed 21 July 2022.

Pennington, Jr., Kenneth J. "Bartolome de Las Casas and the Tradition of Medieval Law". Church History, Vol. 39 (2) (June), pp. 149-161. 1970https://www.jstor.org/stable/3163383 Accessed 21 July 2022

"Renaissance Man" https://www.britannica.com/topic/Renaissance-man Accessed 25 July 2022.

Rubiés, Joan Pau. "Travel Writing and Ethnography". *The Cambridge Companion to Travel Writing*. Ed. Peter Hulme and Tim Youngs. Cambridge UP. 242-260. 2002.

Wilkinson, Maurice. "Fray Bartolome De Las Casas". Blackfriars. (January)Vol. 7, No. 70 pp. 39-45. 1926 https://www.jstor.org/stable/43810581 Accessed 18 July 2022.

Youngs, Tim. *The Cambridge Introduction to Travel Writing*. Cambridge UP, 2013.

A Short Bio of Assoc. Prof. Dr. Gül KOÇSOY

F. Gül Koçsoy graduated from the Department of English Language and Literature at Ataturk University in Erzurum. She completed her MA on Katherine Anne Porter's short fiction and her Doctorate on Willa Cather's novels. After her graduation from the university, she worked as an English teacher for four years in Erzurum and as an instructor at Karadeniz Technical University in Trabzon. Currently, she works as an Associate Prof. Dr. at Firat University in Elazig, Turkey. Her research interests are American culture and literature.

Using Travel Writing as an Authentic Text in EFL Classes

Assist. Prof. Dr. Aysel DEREGÖZÜ

Abstract

Course books play a major role in language teaching and learning, as they are a primary resource for teachers and learners. They consist of contrived materials, mostly simplified texts which should be used in class. However, learners need to be prepared for real life. Hence, in language learning learners should encounter the real-life language use in the target language. The use of authentic material might be contributory for this aim. In this context, this study outlines the importance of authentic writing in EFL classes and how travel writing can be implemented in a process- oriented way in EFL writing classes.

Key Words: Course books, Language teaching, Learners, Target language, Travel writing.

Introduction

Course books are key components of a language classroom. Well-designed course books have a number of recognizable benefits for teachers and learners since they reduce the time needed for lesson preparation, provide a visible and coherent program of work, make standardized instruction possible, provide support, and are a convenient resource for learners. Moreover, they are visually appealing, cultural artifacts and course book packages contain "a wealth of extra material" (McGrath 5-6). Thus, course books support and complement the teacher as well as the learner. However, "It has long been recognized that the language presented to students in textbooks is a poor representation of the real thing, 'far away from that real, informal kind of English which is used very much more than any other during a normal speaking lifetime' (Crystal and Davy 2, qtd. in Gilmore 98) and although more recently much has been done to redress the balance, there remain numerous gaps." (Gilmore 98-99).

Over the past time still, there have been ongoing efforts to develop course books. "However, these textbooks still do not fulfill the learners' needs for communication skills. The reason for this may be the lack of authentic texts that reflect the communicative situations in societies that use English as a first language, such as the UK or the USA." (Allehyani, Burnapp and Wilson 4).

1. English Language Teaching Course Books and the Issue of Authenticity

"It has been argued that explicit teaching of language through contrived examples and texts helps the learners by focusing their processing energies on the target feature, and this is what most course books typically do. However, many SLA researchers argue that this overprotects learners and does not prepare them for the reality of language use outside the classroom. Such researchers as Little et al., Bacon and Finneman, Kuo, McGarry, Wong et al., Nuttall, Mishan, Gilmore and Rilling and Dantas-Whitney argue that authentic materials can provide meaningful exposure to the language as it is actually used, motivate learners and help them develop a range of communicative competencies and enhance positive attitudes towards the learning of a language." (qtd. in Tomlinson 161).

The importance of using authentic material in language classes raises the question of what authenticity means. In the literature, there are many debates on the meaning of authenticity. According to Gilmore (98), at least eight possible inter-related meanings emerge from the literature:

1. The language produced by native speakers for native speakers in a particular language community (Porter and Roberts; Little et al.);
2. The language produced by a real speaker/writer for a real audience, conveying a real message (Morrow; Porter and Roberts; Swaffar; Nunan; Benson and Voller);
3. The qualities bestowed on a text by the receiver, in that it is not seen as something inherent in a text itself but is imparted on it by the reader/listener (Widdowson; Breen);
4. The interaction between students and teachers is a 'personal process of engagement' (van Lier 128);
5. The types of task chosen (Breen; Bachman; van Lier; Benson and Voller; Lewkowicz; Guariento and Morley);
6. The social situation of the classroom (Breen; Arnold; Lee; Guariento and Morley; Rost);
7. Assessment (Bachman; Bachman and Palmer; Lewkowicz);

8. Culture, and the ability to behave or think like a target language group in order" to be recognized and validated by them (Kramsch).

Out of these meanings, Gilmore (98) inferred that "the concept of authenticity can be situated in either the text itself, in the participants, in the social or cultural situation and purposes of the communicative act, or some combination of these."

On the effects of using authentic materials in language classes exist diverse views in the literature. "Many writers claim that authentic materials motivate learners because they are intrinsically more interesting or stimulating than artificial or non-authentic materials (Allwright 179; Freemann and Holden 67; Little and Singleton 124; qtd. in Peacock 144). "Besides the affective advantages of a high-interest factor for motivation, authentic texts capitalize on the alternative knowledge schemes which students possess; they thus have potential advantages for cognitive processing which sanitized texts do not possess." (Swaffar 18). Moreover, "Authentic materials are culturally rich and thus more interesting (Bacon), and they can give students direct access to the cultural information need and help them use the target language authentically (Rogers and Medley)" (qtd. in Barekat and Nobakhti 1060).

"Far fewer authors maintain that authentic materials reduce learner motivation because they are too difficult (Williams 187, 26; Freemann and Holden 68, Morrison 15, qtd. in Peacock 144). Therefore, "Guariento and Morley claim that at post-intermediate levels, the use of authentic materials is advantageous. It is probably because, at these levels, most students know a wide range of vocabulary and all of the structures. Accordingly, they claim that at lower levels, the use of authentic materials may discourage and frustrate students since they lack enough lexical items and structures necessary for dealing with authentic materials." (qtd. in Barekat and Nobakhti 1060). However, it is recommended, "(...) that teachers of adult EFL to beginners try appropriate authentic materials in their classroom, as they may increase their learners' level of on-task behavior, concentration and involvement in the target activity more than artificial materials." (Peacock 152).

However, despite how diverse the view on the effects of using authentic materials in a language class is, a great deal of empirical research pointed to the significance of using them by indicating positive effects on learning. Beresova's study, based on the assumption that authentic materials enhance language acquisition and cultural awareness more significantly than pedagogically modified materials, indicated that authentic materials are more appropriate for advanced L2 readers than pedagogically modified texts. Further, it is stated that "This experiment has proved that using authentic literary texts is to the benefit of the students as they are more enjoyable and students find a chance to interact with the language and its use, and are informed about what is happening in the world they are likely to be interested in." (Beresova 200).

Varmış Kılıç and Genç İlter's study on the change in students' attitudes towards English courses when using authentic material revealed that the control group had a positive effect on the attitudes towards English courses. Reyes used authentic listening activities to determine students' listening comprehension development. He found that most of the participants showed an improvement in listening comprehension. Hence, studies reveal that authentic materials have positive effects on learning.

In this regard, Tomlinson (162) emphasizes that every text that learners encounter should be authentic and that most tasks should be authentic too – otherwise, the learners are not being prepared for the reality of language use. As stated before, the importance of using authentic materials in language classes is crucial to prepare learners for real life.

In language teaching and learning, course books are primary resources. However, it is pointed out that using course books inside the classroom creates a gap between what learners learn in the classroom and real-life English because course books present artificial materials (Guo, qtd. in Allehyani et al. 2). Thus "In addition to the carefully controlled and sequenced language of drills, activities, and contrived passages found in commercially prepared instructional materials, students must also experience the language as it exists naturally, without the "pedagogical processing" so prevalent in most textbooks." (Rogers and Medley 467).

2. Authentic Writing in EFL Classes

In foreign language teaching the ultimate aim is to foster learners' communicative competence in the target language. Communicative competence encompasses productive and receptive skills. As a productive skill, writing has a special importance for individuals' life as "Effective writing skills are central both in higher education and in the world of work that follows" (Kellog and Raulerson 237). "A large share of the value added by businesses in a knowledge-based economy is codified in written documents, placing a premium on a literate workforce (Brandt; qtd. in Kellog and Raulerson 237). Besides that, "Writing experts also agree that if you explore your thoughts and feelings about new information in writing, it helps to make these thoughts and feelings part of your own thinking, which in turn helps you to learn about them (Sebranek et al., qtd. in Westervelt 9).

However, the development of writing skills is a challenging issue for language learners as writing is a complex process, which demands to utilize linguistic patterns of which they are uncertain and transform them into cohesive texts. Furthermore, as authors they have to solve the content problem of what to say and the rhetorical problem of how to say it (Bereiter and Scardamalia; Scardamalia and Bereiter; qtd. in Kellog and Raulerson 238). Hence both cognitive and lingusitic strategies are required to compose a text. Therefore, writing is mainly regarded to be a process, which needs to be practiced in a process – oriented way. In addition to that, as Deqi (70) emphasizes "Writing is also a social and cultural practice, that implies that writing is not simply a matter of manipulating some activities of a universal cognitive process such as pre – writing, drafting, revising, and editing but above all "a means of connecting people with each other in ways that carry particular social meanings" (Hyland 7, qtd. in Deqi 70).

Hence, it can be concluded that written texts are shaped by cultural and social practices and writing tasks have to consider both social and cultural aspects. From this point of view, for language learners writing is a two – facetted matter. At the one hand, they have their own cultural and social backgrounds that shape their way of thinking and text generation, on the other hand, the texts presented to them in language education represent texts produced by a society having their own way of thinking and text generation. This two – facetted perspective of language learners have been neglected widely in course books, as "their main focus is on linguistic substance rather than on the provisions of acquisition and development" (Tomlinson). Thus, "teaching English should be carried out with a practical focus on the learners' culture and context rather than mere instilling western standards to all individuals in all circumstances and places" (Ahmad and Shah 13).

The incorporation of authenticity as well as in texts that represent the target culture and text tasks for learners considering their own writing culture may prevent the one sided perspective in language education.

3. The Use of Travel Writing as an Authentic Writing Task in EFL Classes

As stated before, the use of authentic texts in language education might help learners to encounter the language, as it exists naturally. In this regard, the use of travel writing texts might enable learners to explore real–life language in an engaging way. Travel writing texts are "primarily non-fiction writings about travel, although fictive elements can also be used for narrative purposes, which can be published on a range of platforms, including print media, such as books, guides, and magazines, to digital media, such as e-books and blogs" (McWha et al. 1403). Especially the diversity of travel writing which ranges from "objectively factual guidebooks to much more whimsical short stories or imaginative novels" (McWha et al. 1402) and the diverse platforms on which they are published makes travel writing suitable to use them as a basis for writing activities in foreign language education. Moreover, the diverse text types and platforms on which they are published, such as books, guides, magazines, e-books, and blogs, make them practical to use. Another fact is that travel writers "write for a range of different purposes, including travel promotion, entertainment, inspiration, and personal development, as well as diverse audiences, ranging from the self to close friends and family and on to larger, more commercial or amorphous reader groups " (McWha et al. 1402-1403). Thus, appealing to the interests of diverse readers.

With travel writing, students are exposed to other cultures and experience the world from the eyes of the travel writers. These texts might also encourage learners to write down their own travel experiences. And it is also clear that traveling means not just to travel around the world and visit far away countries, it means also to travel in the own country or in the surrounding of the residential area. Hence, the learners can write their own travel adventures without the need to move to distant places.

But, writing in a foreign language is a challenging process, as learners need to possess a repertoire of lexical, grammatical, orthographic and syntactical knowledge in the target language. Hence, the travel writing intention needs to supported and guided by the teacher. In this regard, the Process Approach Model might help learners in creating their text. With this way of writing "Students can connect to the learning process while experiencing the writing process because they draw on their own ideas as they choose what to write about (Sudol and Sudol) and because they are given time to write, they can experience choices that real-world authors experience (Atwell)" (Westervelt 9).

The Process Approach Model comprises of eight stages (Steele, qtd. in Hasan and Akhand 79):

1. Brainstorming: Generating ideas by brainstorming and discussion.
2. Planning/Structuring: Students exchange ideas into note form and judge quality and usefulness of the ideas.

3. Mind Mapping: Students organize ideas into a mind map, spidergram, or linear form. This stage helps to make the hierarchical relationship of ideas which helps students with the structure of their texts.
4. Writing the first draft: Students write the first draft. This is done in the class frequently in pairs or groups.
5. Peer feedback: Drafts are exchanged, so that students become the readers of each others work. By responding as readers students develop awareness of the fact that a writer is producing something to be read by someone else and thus they can improve their own drafts.
6. Editing: Drafts are returned and improvements are made based upon peer feedback.
7. Final draft: A final draft is written.
8. Evaluation and teachers' feedback: Students' writings are evaluated and teachers provide a feedback on it.

By using the Process Approach Model (Steele, qtd. in Hasan and Akhand 79), learners are guided during the writing process step by step, so that the quality of the product increases, and learners are not frustrate of a challenging writing task.

In the example of writing a text on a travel experience, the first step according to the Process Approach Model would be brainstorming on the topic – in this case the place and what to write about that place. The next phase is on planning and structuring the ideas and notes in a meaningful way. This stage is also quite close with the mind mapping stage where learners outline a hierarchical relationship between their ideas to build the structure of their text. Hence, in the second and third stage the students compile their ideas and structure their text. The next step is to write the draft version of the text in pairs or groups. By this way the challenges of writing in a foreign language are minimalized. After the draft version is created, with peer feedback texts are exchanged and improvements are made. Lastly, the final draft of the travel writing text is written and the teacher gives feedback on the texts, which are a last time revised and completed.

By this way of teaching, an authentic writing task can be created which is based on a travel experience and learners are encouraged to share their impressions and feelings. This type of teaching a foreign language would also contribute to create an authentic learning environment in the language classes.

Bibliography

Allehyani, Badr, et al. "A Comparison of Teaching Materials (School Textbooks vs Authentic Materials) from the Perspective of English Teachers and Educational Supervisors in Saudi Arabia." *International Journal of English Language and Linguistics Research*, vol. 5, no. 2, 2017, pp.1-14.

Ahmad, Hussain, and Shah, Sayyed Rashid. "English Textbooks and Cultural Attitudes of Saudi EFL Learners: Investigating Teachers' Perspectives." *VFAST Transactions on Education and Social Sciences*, vol. 5, no. 1, 2014, pp.12-20.

Barekat, Behzad, and Nobakhti, Hamed. "The Effect of Authentic and Inauthentic Materials in Cultural Awareness Training on EFL Learners' Listening Comprehension Ability." *Theory and Practice in Language Studies*, vol. 4, no. 5, 2014, pp. 1058-1065.

Beresova Jana. "Authentic Materials – Enhancing Language Acquisition and Cultural Awareness." *Procedia - Social and Behavioral Sciences*, vol. 192, 2015, pp. 195 – 204.

Deqi, Zeng. "The Process-Oriented Approach to ESL/EFL Writing Instruction and Research." *Celea Journal*, vol. 28, no. 5, 2005, pp. 66-70.

Gilmore, Alex. "Authentic Materials and Authenticity in Foreign Language Learning." *Language Teaching*, vol. 40, 2007, pp.97–118.

Hasan, Md. Kamrul, and Akhand, Mohd. Moniruzzaman. "Approaches to Writing in EFL/ESL Context: Balancing Product and Process in Writing Class at Tertiary Level." *Journal of NELTA*, vol. *15,* no. 1-2, 2011, pp. 77–88. https://doi.org/10.3126/nelta.v15i12.4612

Kellog, Ronald T., and Raulerson, Bascom A. "Improving the Writing Skills of College Students." *Psychonomic Bulletin & Review*, vol. 14, no. 2, 2007, pp. 237-242.

McGrath, Ian (2013). *Teaching Materials and The Roles of EFL/ ESL Teachers. Practice and Theory*. Bloomsbury, 2013.

McWha, Madelene, et al.. "Travel Writers and the Nature of Self: Essentialism, Transformation and (Online) Construction". *Annals of Tourism Research*, 2017, pp.14 24.

Peacock, Matthew. "The Effect of Authentic Materials on the Motivation of EFL Learners". *ELT Journal*, vol. 51 no. 2, 1997, pp.144 – 156.

Reyes, C. A. Z. "The Impact of Using Authentic Materials to Promote Listening Comprehension in 4th Grade Students". Thesis. 2017.

Rogers, Carmen Villegas, and Medley, Frank W. Jr. "Language with a Purpose: Using Authentic Materials in the Foreign Language Classroom." *Foreign Language Annals*, vol. 5, no. 21, 1988, pp. 467– 476.

Swaffar, Janet. "Reading Authentic Texts in a Foreign Language: A Cognitive Model." *The Modern Language Journal*, vol. 69, no. 1, 1985, pp.15-34.

Tomlinson, Brian. "Materials Development For Language Learning And Teaching." *Language Teaching*, vol. 45, no.2, 2012, pp.143–179.

Varmış Kılıç, Zerhan, and Genç İlter, Binnur. "The Effect of Authentic Materials on 12th Grade Students' Attitudes in EFL Classes." *ELT Research Journal*, vol. 4, no. 1, 2015, pp. 2-15.

Westervelt, Lisa. "Teaching Writing Using the Process-Oriented Approach." 1998, https://files.eric.ed.gov/fulltext/ED420864.pdf

A Short Bio of Assist. Prof. Dr. Aysel DEREGÖZÜ

Aysel Deregözü is an Assistant Professor Doktor at the Education Faculty, English Language Teaching of Inonu University. She received her Ph.D. degree in Foreign Language Education, German Language Teaching from Marmara University. Language teaching methods, language teacher education and literature are her fields of interest.

Inner and Outer Voyages into the Contested Spaces of Cultural Memory in Jack Kerouac's *On the Road*

Assist. Prof. Dr. Dilek Ünügür ÇALIŞKAN

Abstract

On the Road (1957), by Jack Kerouac, depicts sex, drug, and youth-obsessed American culture that opposed the conformism of the time and reflects the intellectual environment of the 1940s and 1950s youth (sub) culture, a much-studied topic (started in the 1930s). Through the inner and outer voyages, he presents the carefully constructed and contested (mental and geographical) spaces of cultural Memory to show the existence of various subcultures and the need to study their relations to the dominant culture. Kerouac rewriting the American story anew shows the emptiness and the bankruptcy of Capitalism, Manifest Destiny, American Democracy, and Identity that create madness. He presents a counter-image, a (mad) dean Moriarty mirroring the emptiness of this success and progress-based identity committing visible and invisible crimes. Decentering the concept; of the Normal American, the Little Man based on WASP, God, Capitalism, Masculinity, Family, America as a heaven, and so on, Kerouac presents a new spirituality via the journey of Jazz Music (Slavery). He also criticizes the conflicting perspectives of behaviorism and psychoanalysis. The addictive relationship of Sal Paradise with mad Dean Moriarty, the New American Saint, illustrates all the turmoil and pressure on young people in their struggle to forge a true-self Identity (both as an individual and a writer). This study, at the same time, will explore the novel in the light of the anti-psychiatrist R. D. Laing's view of madness, mad society, and counter/sub-culture investigated by Jack Kerouac via the inner and outer voyages into the mental and geographical spaces of the cultural memory.

Keywords: Madness, Counter/subculture, Inner and Outer Voyages, Identity, Cultural Memory

Introduction

On the Road by Jack Kerouac, written in 1947 and published in 1957, criticizes the taboos and hypocrisy surrounding sex, race, and gender in contemporary capitalistic American culture and presents a new spirituality based on difference and diversity. In opposition to the conformism of the day, *On the Road* depicts sex, drug, and youth-obsessed American culture representing the intellectual milieu of the young subculture of the 1940s and 1950s, the Beats. *On the Road* emphasizes the need for examination of the mental (health) spaces of the young. It is a call for understanding. The New Saint, mad criminal Dean Moriarty, as a counter figure, mirrors the emptiness and shallowness of the American Identity based on progress and success stories via the inner and outer voyages into the mental spaces of the young and geographical places like the city, farmlands, corn fields, deserts, and the rivers examining the North and the South, the East and the West of the country and encountering subcultural groups during his journeys accompanied with hunger, delusions, madness, and crime. Kerouac writes about the importance of writing for political and spiritual change. It is up to Sal Paradise --with the pun on his name how to sell America as a haven--to establish a healthy weltanschauung through his observation and travel experience and to initiate into the society (of healthy intellectuals). Kerouac (the Beats) opens up a space for new debates related to the youth sub/cultures of black people and people of color in their relation to women and the dominant culture by presenting the masculine, misogynistic and capitalist Dean Moriarty (a car parking expert) and his dependent Sal Paradise.

The Beats, also known as Beatnik, a satirical term hated by Beats and coined by a newspaper reporter combining the word Beat with the word Sputnik the Russian satellite recently launched: consisted of a group of New Wave writers, artists, and poets, specifically Kerouac, Allen Ginsberg, and a few others. It is the best example showing the anger and labeling given to a subculture or a generation making them into stereotypes, reducing the Beat into a young man in a beret, dressed in black, wearing a goatee, and allergic to the idea of holding a job down, to put them down. The term, Beat, as explained by Kerouac, originally refers to the word "Beatific" or "Beatitude" and means "I'm beat!" In a society that values heterosexuality, whiteness, sameness, and consumption, Kerouac depicts in his novel *On the Road* the anger and antagonism toward youth, the most researched subject in America in the 1930s. Although criticized by media for their negativity and "affirmation of death" rather than "the affirmation of life," *On the Road* is a plea and a call for a healthy outlook related to "difference" (also in writing). As defined in the article

"On the Holy Road: The Beat Movement as Spiritual Protest" by Prothero, there are two tendencies by critics and by popular magazines to view the movement "narrowly as a literary cultural impulse" or "as an inclination to judge this impulse negatively as a revolt against rather a protest for something" (205):

> Life claimed they were at war with things sacred in Eisenhower's America-"Mom, Dad, Politics, Marriage, Savings Bank, Organized Religion, Literary Elegance, Law, the Ivy Suit and Higher Education, to say nothing of the Automatic Dishwasher, the Cellophane-wrapped Soda Cracker, the Split-Level House and the or peace-provoking H-bomb."[5] The Nation dismissed the beats as sayers"; even Playboy called them the "nihilists."[6] (205-206)

Like transcendentalism, which is a religious revolt against corpse-cold Unitarian orthodoxy, as affirmed by Miller, the beat movement is a spiritual protest against the moribund orthodoxies of 1950s America (Prothero 208). American religious historians were uninterested in this newly presented spirituality and limited it to some labels of Zen with no true Zen orthodoxy (207). On the contrary, according to Prothero," the beats were spiritual protesters as literary innovators and ought, therefore, to be viewed at least as characters in the drama of American religion" (208). Their new outlook reflects the search for mental health care and the difficulty of constructing an authentic self-identity (as a writer) in the so-called big American family. Sal's obsession with the fatherless mad Dean in On the Road is a metaphor for the desire and need for belonging. As expressed by Allen Johnson, "the analogy between capitalism and addiction becomes a leitmotif in Beat writing" (110). Dean is boxer-like. As mentioned by Elsa Devienne, for exercise enthusiasts, fitness entrepreneurs, and physicians, muscularity was a sign of strength and manliness. These qualities were considered essential for fighting against communism (320) and is to beat Marxism down, as suggested by the German name Carlo, meaning warrior, Marx alluding to (Karl Marx) Marxism. Torn apart between the two warring ideologies of capitalism (Dean Moriarty) and communism (Carlo Marx) in the Golden Age of Capitalism in Cold War America, Sal is "housed" in an apartment on Colfax Avenue. The Avenue alludes to the Gold Rush Days, and the Golden Road is associated with materialism and the pursuit of happiness. It will never be possible for young people to settle down and be happy. Progress is a conflicting idea that pushes young men to move from one city to another and to become restless and competitive. And in the Cold War America, they should take their side by the Nation against communism:

> And in the back of my mind was the wild thought, Where is Dean and what is he doing right now? Chad had decided not be Dean's friend any more, for some odd reason, and he even didn't even know where he lived. "Is Carlo Marx in town?" "Yes." But he wasn't talking to him any more either. This was the beginning of Chad King's withdrawal from our general gang. ... The word was that Tim Gray had an apartment waiting for me up Colfax Avenue, That Roland Mayor was already living in it and was waiting for me to join him. I sensed some kind of conspiracy in the air, and this conspiracy lined up two groups in the gang: it was Chad King and Tim Gray and Roland Major, together with Rawlinses, generally agreeing to ignore Dean Moriarty and Carlo Marx: I was smack in the middle of this interesting war. It was a war with social overtones. (Kerouac 38)

Three figures led the beat movement: a working-class French-Canadian Catholic from Lowell, Massachusetts (Kerouac), a middle-class Russian-American Jew from Paterson, New Jersey (Ginsberg), and an upper-class Anglo-American Protestant from St. Louis (Burroughs) began with the meeting of Kerouac, Burroughs, Ginsberg in New York in 1944. The new movement coursed its way with a large supporting group of novelists, poets, and hangers-on through the San Francisco poetry renaissance of the 1950s into the 1960s. The men's gang united with a new consciousness; and a new vision, rejected dominant spiritual norms, and established religious institutions (Kerouac 209). The beats shared an undefined commitment to a spiritual search; in the form of pilgrimage, as expressed by Prothero:

> They aimed not arrive but to travel and, in the process, to transform into sacred space every back alley through which they ambled and every tenement in which they lived. Thus the beats appear in their lives and in their novels not only pilgrims but also as heroes (and authors) of quest tales, wandering (and writing) bhikkhus who scour the earth in a never fully satisfied attempt to find a place to rest. (211)

Like Kerouac, in search of spiritual rest, defining himself as a haunted sick child at six in one of his autobiographical writings (Johnson 49), experienced a similar challenge as a young boy and later a writer. His attempt to join the Naval Air Force also failed in 1942. They were moving from one house into another in flight to escape the memories of the death of his brother Gabriel and the publishing process (nine years) of his book; the gang members in *On the Road*, too, are affected by a war with social overtones. The American Way of Life, as explained by the American critic and writer Joyce Carol Oates, "is based on the big American Dream, which is a false dream of conquest, control, and ownership. It is an impossible dream of overcoming mutability"(Creighton 107). Similarly, for Kerouac, it is ghostly, haunted and nightmarish. America became a consumer paradise after the World War II. An American century with an ever-rising Gross National Product, expanding highway program, and mushrooming suburban shopping malls where the credit card was a sign of class distinctions (Hoffman 5). By the 1950s, a stream of criticism about material conditions and the quality of media started. The only concern was the welfare of the homogenous white middle-class suburban society, which suffered from too much consumption.

The "Fair Employment Practices (FEP) laws passed between 1945 and 1964 by 28 states could not mask racial discrimination that remained pervasive in the North (Kazin 926)." The plight of people of color and blacks in the South and ghettos of northern cities remained unseen until the civil rights movements of the late 1950s and the ghetto risings in the middle 1960s. Not only the West but also the East was wild, as Sal painfully comes to know. Starving and hallucinating in Harrisburg (Harry's Ferry or Louisburg), a city he loathes, The Ghost of Susquehanna teaches him a life lesson. The city Harrisburg was taken from (Susquehanna) Indians after a license (1705) to trade by an Englishmen, John Harris, a trading post and ferry service. It became a scene for the National Tariff Convention of 1827 and the first national Whig convention (1839), the center of transportation after the opening of the Pennsylvania Canal (1834) and the arrival of the first railroad train (1836) (Britannica). Kerouac connects existence to home and the body, which becomes a ghostly and haunting existence. Home and the city become the extension of the body. The city ghostly exists only in imagination, memory, and phantasy:

> No, there is a wilderness in the East; it's the same wilderness Ben Franklin plodded in the oxcart days when he was a postmaster, the same as it was when George Washington was a wild-buck Indian-fighter, when Daniel Boone told stories by Pennsylvania lamps and promised to find a Gap, when Bradford built his road and men whooped her up in log cabins. There were not great Arizona spaces for the little man, just the bushy wilderness of eastern Pennsylvania, Maryland, and Virginia, the backroads, the black-tar roads that curve among the mournful rivers like Susquehanna, Monongahela, old Potomac and Monocacy. That night I had to sleep in Harrisburg I had to sleep in the railroad station on a bench; at dawn the station masters threw me out. ... isn't it true that you start your life a sweet child believing in everything under your father's roof? Then comes the day of the Laodiceans, when you know you are wretched and

> miserable and poor and blind and naked, and with the visage of a gruesome grieving ghost you go shuddering through nightmare life ... But the madman drove me home to New York ... (Kerouac105-107)

The city alludes to the cyclic and delusional nature of time, memory, and the colonial history of North America: wilderness, massacre, genocide, death, exploitation, hunger, and pain, metaphorically experienced by Sal at the train station. Kerouac presents an environmental or 'geographical' vision connected to existential and phenomenological traditions and analyzes the instances of trauma and madness, but ends up brought back to New York by a madman. He concentrates on time-space situatedness like the anti-psychiatrist R. D. Laing. Sal connects his body to place (city) and his home as an extension of his body and others. As stated by McGeachan,

> ... in order to explore the private worlds Laing and Esterson ... Not only were they attempting to engage in assessing the intricate behavior existing between family members in a variety of combinations, but they were also attempting to move away from the artificial setting of the mental institution into the place from which the person originally came: the home. The environment of home was hence a key factor, and the two men were acutely aware of how important this space was for the people they were treating. (286)

Laing's attention which was on experience and existential analysis of action sought answers related to the connection between behavior and individual's experience in interpersonal relations and the effect of one person on another (287). In a nexus of others imagined dreamed, fantasied or 'real', Laing's concern was to expand accounts of experience and action in imagination, dream and phantasy (286),

> ... in order to achieve an authentic social identity an individual must not only have an identity-for-self but also an identity for others, given that these two forms of identity cannot be divorced from one another. This claim indicates that one's self-identity is always reliant upon one's own experience of the other in numerous complex forms, ... when attempting to compose an account of a person, one must be constantly aware that each person is always acting upon others but also being acted upon by others. (287).

Sal's existence is dependent on others, Dean, Hassel, and those he meets on the 'road,' at home. The American society symbolized by the imaginary characters Sal and the other gang members who are severely dependent on mad Dean (capitalistic ideology) and his actions in a network of crime, violence, passion, desire and love relationship, such representing the micro geopolitics of the time and the macro geography of America. Like Laing's work into families and experimental spaces of mental health care, the mental health of young people are examined by Kerouac through a geographical lens as Sal sits on the old broken–down river pier at the end of the novel thinking about Dean, and his lost father Old Dean Moriarty openning an important debate related to the problem of youth and young writers. This study will explore the novel in the light of the anti-psychiatrist R. D. Laing's view of madness and mad society, and counter/sub culture and the mental health (spaces) of the young investigated by Jack Kerouac, through experimentation, the characters' interaction with each other (each representing ideas related to race, ethnicity, and gender) in their relation to Dean Moriarty and the American landscape.

Adolescence, Youth, Culture, Counterculture, and the Beats

Jack Kerouac in *On the Road* highlights the importance of a healthy initiation into the society. And he wishes to be transformed into an adolescent person. Adolescence is a difficult period open for discussion. The age one enters adolescence is getting lower, whereas the age for becoming a mature adult gets higher, and the adolescence period is expanded (Berger 12). Therefore forming a mature and long-lasting worldview can take a long time, even for intellectuals. The "youthful" functions of student life hinder maturity (Berger 12). When compared evidence from European and American novels about groups of young people "struggling to find themselves" show; a George Eliot or Dostoevsky novel portrays a mature, articulate or aware character of twenty or twenty-one (or even eighteen) whereas a contemporary American novel depicts young persons in their late twenties or in their late thirties. There is an extension of "youthfulness" in American culture. "Americans are members of the 'younger generation' from the time they begin to stay out at night to the time they begin to grow bald and arthritic, and find the stairs steeper, and the co-eds younger looking" as mentioned by Bennet M. Berger (13). The cultural life of the United States is centralized when compared to most European nations (14).

As noted in Brake, the young are affected by economic, educational, and occupational changes at specific historical junctures; class and generation (31) and the period between 1930 and 1950 is particularly critical for the young in Europe and in the United States in terms of scientific, ideological and religious perspectives related to education, mental health and hygiene. Therefore, youth and youth culture are controversial terms still open to debate and need careful approach. As Brake states according to Matza, youth is a time of rebellion, delinquency, radicalism, and bohemianism (31), the sociological explanation, “the adolescents lived in a different world from the adults, creating an inclusive social order separated from adult society" of Reuters in 1934 at Yale captured scientists attention (47–48). The phrase "youth culture," invented by Parsons in 1942, describes the intersection of age and sex and fosters values that are counter to those of the adult world, like productive work and adherence to routine and responsibility (Brake 48). His perspective contends that adolescents acquire values related to spending, decadent pastimes, and irresponsibility.

In the 1950s, middle-class adolescent culture with an embrace of academic performance replaced rebelliousness with sullen seclusion as the emphasis shifted. The young person was given more freedom and grew fiercely committed to their organization, dating people of the opposite sex, cult leaders, and folk heroes. Success in manly strength replaced academic achievement. Middle-class kids used alcohol and sexual activity to signal their freedom from adult supervision and help them integrate into society (Brake 48/49). Working-class youth rebelled against the institution of learning by engaging in delinquency and skipping class staying outside the middle-class ideal of success (49-49). *On the Road* alludes to these obsessive youth studies of the 30s by portraying youth culture in America, depicting the existential concerns of young people around and over the age of thirty, as the age range also differs in America. The term "youth culture" has been loosely applied to a structural monolith of those under thirty, regardless of class, age group, ethnicity, or gender. There is a complex kaleidoscope of adolescent and youth subcultures with various age groups and lifestyles.

Therefore, there is a need to look at the definition of subculture and culture and their relation. Culture is a repository for signs, or potential meaning structures, that actors can inherit or reject. Under their very existence, subcultures imply that there are additional modes of cultural expression that reflect the diversity of a culture, which frequently appears to the untrained eye to predominate among the populace. The subcultures are closely related to the parent class culture and appeal to various self-images, values, and behaviors. In these subcultures, myth, and reality coexist harmoniously. Culture exists on several degrees; the historical level of ideas, the values, meaning, the consequences of the maternal production process, and the symbolic and material effects of artifacts and mass media on cultures. Human action as a dynamic, subjective component is dependent on perception. Subcultures are anywhere there is a recognized and organized constellation of values, behavior, and deeds that deviate from the prevailing norms. As a "collective solution," subcultures are defined as "meaning systems, modes of expression, or lifestyles developed by groups in subordinate structural positions in response to dominant meaning systems. They reflect their attempt to resolve structural contradictions." Subcultures defined as "meaning systems, modes of expression, or lifestyles" are developed by groups in subordinate structural positions in response to dominant meaning systems (Brake 7-8)

At the existential level, subculture indicates how meanings are taken from subculture to project an image/identity: as the subculture has to develop new group meanings and form a constellation of behavior, action, and values that have meaningful symbolism for the actors involved and at the sociological level, it offers an understanding of human interaction against a cultural and symbolic background with its active role in the reconstruction between structure and actor; at the structural level, it shows how culture is mediated to and generated by a collectivity of social actors (Brake 9). Meanings taken from subcultures affect the internal labeling of identity by using external symbols to develop a self-image with a cultural and existential reality (Brake 9). In *On the Road*, the imaginary cultural rebel Dean Moriarty trans-passing the realm between dream/vision and reality existing in myth/reality in the history and culture of America has to be made visible. Described as a youth in the novel," He was simply a youth tremendously excited with life, and though he was a con-man, he was only conning because he wanted so much to live and to get involved with people who would otherwise pay no attention to him" (Kerouac 7). Dean is a con man committing crimes for a society to exist.

As mentioned by Sal (39), he is a criminal with a Denver record for stealing cars and going to the reformatory (between the ages of eleven -to seventeen). Jack Kerouac opens up a new cultural space for adolescence and the initiation period with the prophet-like Dean in American culture and literature to discuss the problem of youth in multicultural America, whose madness Sal's aunt carefully observes. Hall suggests young people can solve problems in an imaginary way; Kerouac, too, presents the battle of young people with the dominant culture when their class position, class access to education, and occupation are considered (Brake 6).

Several cultures, not homogenous, develop in the context of the dominant value system and require constant modifications and adaptations of dominant values and ideas as they share elements of the parent culture. In this context, membership is synonymous with membership to a class culture and its extension of the subculture (which can also be an adaptation or an opposition to the class system), which reflects a 'subordinate value system' that presents no alternatives but negotiations with the dominant value systems. It means a "pragmatic acceptance" of hegemony or a "corporate culture" that emerges from them. Subcultural groups hold mixed values situating them to the group's specific class context or subgroup problems: They take over styles that are placed in the family or neighborhood or mediated from the synthetic culture of the teenage entertainment industry or expressing dominant meaning systems. Subcultures are not deviant or oppositional, although they may be rebellious, which never reaches a hinged opposition (6-7).

Therefore, Sal Paradise and all the gang members admire Dean Moriarty, representing the dominant parent culture, where ironically, the ''Father'' is absent. As a lost and problematic young, he is in search of a parental figure as a guide. Still a controversial subject in contemporary American youth studies as mentioned by Brake, center around four main areas: respectable youth; conformist or straight youth: delinquent youth; the teenagers reflect the class cultures of their parents; young adolescent males involved with illegal activities like theft, violence, and vandalism and females with sexual misbehavior: cultural rebels usually middle class and with middle-class education involved in subcultures in the fringes of bohemian traditions adherent to literary traditions rather than being artists and politically militant youth; factions of political and broad mass movements, the scope of politics may range from environmental to community politics to direct action (31-32). Ironically, the shiny-minded mad Dean Moriarty, the delinquent youth, and a cultural rebel is at war with politically militant youth, the dark-minded Carlo Marx and Sal Paradise is not able to cope with the two (Koreauc7). Metaphorically, Dean represents American Capitalism; and, Carlo Marx represents Russian Communism, and Sal Paradise represents The Young American Nation in the Cold War. His fictional character Dean, a car thief, and a misogynist-- based on his real friend Neil Cassady-- is described by Sal in the novel as a conning youth who get along well:

> He was conning me and I knew it (for room and board and "how-to-write," etc.), and he knew, I knew (this has been the basis of our relationship), but I didn't care and we got along fine—no pestering, no catering; we tiptoed around each other like heartbreaking new friends. I began to learn from him as much he probably learned from me. As far as my work was concerned he said, "Go ahead, everything you do is great." He watched over my shoulder as I write stories, yelling, Yes, That's right! Wow! Man! and "Phew!" and wiped his face with handkerchief. " Man,

wow, there's so many things to do, so many things to write! How to even *begin* to get it all down and without modified restrains all hung-up on like literary inhibitions and grammatical fears . . . " (7)

Carlo Marx and Old Bull Lee, two of Kerouac's other characters, are modeled after Allen Ginsberg and William Burroughs, respectively. The Beat Generation Jack Kerouac, Neil Cassady, Allen Ginsberg, and William Burroughs as a counterculture of authors who opposed the values and standards of mainstream American culture and its intellectual foundation while giving voice to the silent subcultures of their day. They challenged the long-accepted tenets of American literature with an iconoclastic approach to language as expressed by David Sterritt, in "The Beat Minds of their Generation"(Belasco et al. 1608). So that Jack Kerouac uses the journey metaphor to attack the dominant discourses and the institutions of the American society he is to fit in, as he was born into a French-Canadian family in Lowell, Massachusetts he loves, and spoke joual until he was six years old (1610).

Geography plays a crucial role as an important aspect of identity and the towns appear as characters in his fiction like (Dean) Moriarty, a town in New Mexico. He writes about the family in the consumerist America and examines the ties between the generations, focusing on the young people who are dependent solely on their aunts for support and the absent father or mother, in a nod to the tribal traditions of the indigenous Americans as the novel discusses the theme of initiation, which is a painful one in consumerist American society. "Energized by a booming economy, advances in technology, and new consumer goods that made life more comfortable and enjoyable, at least for some people" (1609) in America, he observes and examines the familial and brotherly relationships by comparing, contrasting and portraying them with the people he meets on the road. The journey with Dean is a metaphor for Manifest Destiny and the so-called American Democracy.

Despite the glamour, as stated by David Sterritt, "the nation's psychological and spiritual health did not keep pace with its material well-being" (Belasco et al. 1609). *On the Road* reflects this madness-inducing consumerist capitalist mad society with the travel stories, Sal's obsessive love of madness (Dean), and the observation of the landscape. This haunted and paranoid society commits invisible crimes by the police and the government, as emphasized by the haunted Sal Paradise, who describes himself as a ghost (Kerouac 17). The prejudices against other subcultural groups are juxtaposed and presented in the "groupthink "of Dean and Sal, the cultural rebels and their gang, white and middle-class.

"Groupthink," a term coined by William H. Whyte, Jr., designates patterns of consensus that are "guided almost totally by the whims and prejudices of the group" (Belasco et al. 1609). The gang also reflects the idea of groupthink in popular and academic discourses of the time. Dean organizes the people around him (Kerouac 38), a metaphor for capitalism and the American way of life. Dean is the organization man, representing popular and academic discourse that started to use terms like "rat race," "lonely crowd," and "organization man" (Belasco et al. 1609). Similarly, the counterculture Beats, reflecting the idea of artistic groupthink, gave birth to a still much-regarded and studied art movement, music, and literature. Though Jack Kerouac invented the term beat, John Clellon Holmes (1952) introduced it in an article written in New York Times Magazine entitled "This is the Beat Generation."

> ... it implies the feeling of having been used, of being raw. It involves a sort of nakedness of mind, and, ultimately, of soul; a feeling of being reduced to the bedrock of consciousness. In short, it means being undramatically pushed up against the wall of oneself. A man is beat whenever he goes for broke and wagers the sum of his resources on a single number; and the young generation has done that continually from early youth. (par. 3)

The (Beats) boys are wild but not lost like the Lost generation, "they drink to 'come down or to 'get high,' not to illustrate anything (par. 6)" and they invent totems and even "God" (par.7). Their excursions into drugs or promiscuity come out of curiosity, not disillusionment (par.6). Beat circle met one another in 1940 at Columbia University, where Kerouac and Ginsberg were studying literature and Burroughs was a psychology and anthropology graduate; with a new approach to the so-called youth culture, they hold up a mirror to the society that dismembers its youth; travel stories in *On the Road* record the youth subcultures of the time, highlighting the difficulty in establishing an authentic self-image and identity and discusses the problem of subcultures in America. In the United States, there are many subcultures (ethnic and racial groups) that unite by sharing the language, food, and customs of their heritage and shared experiences, posing problems for the parent culture. But, as stated by Brake, for Parson (1962), youth interested in activism seek justice and social change but are frustrated because of being deprived of power and influence and "are ready to work within rather than in opposition" (Brake 48).

Dean Moriarty in *On the Road* desperately travels the whole continent to find his father, Old Dean Moriarty. On the other hand, the fatherless Sal seeks fatherly/ brotherly love and care from the restless Dean, who cannot settle down and father his children by Camille and Inez. He represents the degenerated Puritans/Protestants: the capitalistic ideals of America and the class problem. There is a big clash between the ruling class and the other classes, as there is no accepted class consciousness in America; because of the immigrant labor force problem. Different ethnic groups with varying languages and cultural backgrounds ruled by White Anglo-Saxon Protestants elites who tried to impose their own culture absorbed the imposed culture and were happy to find a job and a new home. But with the successive generations facing structural contradictions, the Americanization of low-status groups failed (Brake 30). Subcultures have a crucial role in the dynamics of society as they call the adequacy of the dominant cultural group into question, as the educational system trains youth from lower strata into meaningless, poorly paid, uncreative occupations (30). Therefore, the young people rely on subculture because it offers solution (escape) to their problems, as subcultures are crucial for a self-image and identity.

Subcultures

For Cohen, the subculture offers an imaginary solution (32) like Kerouac's writing: Sal Paradise, a writer, wants to know Dean more and needs new experiences, like Kerouac himself. Dean, although a con-man, seemed to be his long-lost brother despite the differences in their characters (Kerouac 9-10). Although his aunt warned him about Dean, his life (and his learning process) on the road begins with this meeting, which would mix up all his friends and all he left of his family in "a big dust cloud over the American Night."

> Carlo told him of Dean Old Bull Lee, Elmer Hassel, Jane: Lee in Texas Growing weed, Hassel on Riker's Island, Jane wandering on Times Square in a benzedrine hallucination, with her baby girl in her arms and ending up in Bellevue. And Dean told Carlo of unknown people in the West like Tommy Snark, the clubfooted poolhall rotation shark and cardplayer and queer saint. He told him of Roy Johnson, Big Ed Dunkel, his boyhood buddies, his street buddies, his innumerable girls and sex parties and pornographic pictures, his heroes, heroines, adventures. They rushed down the street together, digging everything in the early way they had, which later became so much sadder and perceptive and blank. But then they danced down the streets like dingledodies, and I shambled after as I have been doing all my life after people who interest me, because the only people for me are the mad ones, the ones who are mad to live, mad to talk, mad to be saved, desirous of everything at the same time, the ones who never yawn or say common thing, but burn, burn like fabulous

> yellow roman candles exploding like spiders across the stars and in the middle you see the blue center light pop and everybody goes. Awww! (8)

Dean seemed to have control over the gang, Carlos (communism) and the girls until the time they became enemies, which Sal did not realize when. The youth subcultures that Kerouac presents in his fiction not only tackle the discrepancy between the parent culture and the subcultures it also depicts the fight between the two ideologically fiendish cultures, the war between Capitalism and Russian Communism, and the Post War atmosphere. After having one trip to the South, now Sal is ready to take a journey "to the West for the very first time," but unfortunately instead of going to the West, he seems to be moving to North (12), metaphorically, in search of democracy. Dean, as the western kinsman of the Sun (10), the British Imperialism attacks Carlo Marx, the political rebel in the red afternoon where Sal comes to realize his self and his ghostly existence as America:

> ...I wasn't scared. I was just somebody else, some strange, and my whole life was a haunted life, the life of a ghost. I was halfway across America, at the dividing line between the East of my youth and the West of my future, and maybe that's why it happened right there and then, that strange red afternoon. (16-17)

Dean and Carlo do not belong to the same picture and Sal notices he is like an Italian, a fascist:

> Dean made a profile shot ... I took a straight picture that made me look like a thirty-year-old Italian who'd kill anybody who said anything against his mother. This picture Carlo and Dean neatly cut down the middle with a razor and saved a half each in their wallet. Dean was wearing a real Western business suit for his big trip back to Denver; he'd finished his first thing in New York. I say fling, but he only worked like a dog in parking lots. The most fantastic parking-lot attendant in the world, he can back a car ... (9)

Sal's journey to South is done, representing Black culture symbolized in music, but the West needs to be explored; Los Angeles, the jungle and the loneliest and the most brutal of all cities (Kerouac 85),

> The beatest characters in the country swarmed on the sidewalks—all of it under those soft Southern California stars that are lost in the brown halo of the huge desert encampment LA really is. You could smell tea, weed I mean marijuana, floating in the air, together with the chili beans and beer

that grand sound of bop floated from beer parlors; it mixed medleys with every kind of cowboy and boogie-woogie in the American night. Everybody looked like Hassel Wild negroes with bop caps and goatees came laughing by; then long-haired broken down hipsters straight of Route 66 from New York; then old desert rats, carrying packs and heading for a park bench at the Plaza; then Methodists ministers with raveled sleeves, and an occasional Nature Boy saint in beard and sandal. I wanted to meet them all, talk to everybody, but Terry and I were too busy trying to get a buck together. (86)

Beside the glamor of Hollywood, where Terry and Sal went to try to work in the drugstore at Sunset and Vine, its dark corner is revealed:

> Great families off jalopies from the hinterlands ... gaping for sight of some movie star; and the movie star never showed up. When the limousine passed they rushed eagerly to the curb and ducked to look ... Handsome queer boys who had come to Hollywood to be cowboys walked around, wetting their eyebrows with hincty fingertip. The most beautiful little gals in the world cut by in slacks; they came to be starlets, they ended up in drive-ins. ... Hollywood Boulevard was a great, screaming frenzy of cars; there were minor accidents at least once a minute; everybody was rushing off toward the farthest palm—and beyond that was the desert and nothingness. (86)

The problems of the Native Americans and the Mexican people who lived mainly in Texas, Colorado, New Mexico, Arizona, and California, in other words, the original inhabitants of the land: the farmers and the real owners of the land, which is the Promised Land and the fantastic end of America, remain invisible. Kerouac sheds light on the hinterlands, homosexual boys, etc., and all the subcultures that did not count (82).

> Before 1950 even basic population data upon which to base vital rates were lacking or at best, unreliable. In 1950 data relating to persons of Mexican-American descent were obtained by the Census Bureau by identifying white persons of Spanish surname on the census schedules. These data were published for the five States mentioned previously. The Census Bureau used this same procedure during the 1960 census to identify persons with Spanish surnames (2, 3).... For the past several decades ethnic studies in this country have been limited almost exclusively to the Negro-American or black subculture, to the neglect of other disadvantaged minority groups such as the American Indian or the Mexican-American subcultures. Consequently, a great deal more is

> known about the morbidity and mortality patterns for black Americans as well as for white or Anglo-Americans. (Roberts and Askew 263)

Therefore, there is the need to study these subcultures; Sal's love to Terry, a Mexican girl, a Pachuco wildcat (89) symbolizes his affinity toward Mexican culture, as she is his kind of soul girl who loved love (81) that needs to be known and together they go off to Bakersfield to pick grapes (89) with a plan to hit fruit wholesaler in the town. They would live in tents and pick grapes in the cool California mornings, although Sal doesn't like the idea at all. Unfortunately, they cannot find a job in the Mexican town they sit and drink wine with the hobos and move to Terry's hometown Sabinal to seek a shelter by her brother. Hitchhiking they travel with a truck whose owner is poor. They find refuge in music. The familiar Black music and culture of the time dominating the atmosphere of the book offers identification and refuge for Sal like it did for the white youth.

Jazz, as expressed by Ralph Ellison, "is much more than just musical technique and is, to African American culture, wherein each musician's improvisation "represents . . . a definition of his identity: member of the collectivity and as a link in the chain of tradition (quoted in Malcolm 86) in "'Jazz America': Jazz and African Culture in Jack Kerouac's *On the Road*." In this respect it can be said as mentioned by Dick Hebdige, Jack Kerouac like Norman Mailer carried the idealization of Negro cultures to ludicrous extremes in their novels that could serve for white youth as the model of "freedom-in-bondage" (48), for which Music is crucial, and familiar. There is a tradition of miscegenation in jazz and White youth culture is linked to the black urban working class (47). Later black man developed the difficult to listen and imitate New York sound to restrict white identification. Nevertheless, the 'beat' and the hipster started to improvise their own exclusive style called the 'jazz of pure abstraction' (47). On the other hand, the integration of black and white, led to inevitable controversy related to themes of race, sex and rebellion that lead to a moral panic (47). The mythology of Black Man and his Culture developed. The Negro was blowing free:

> ...untouched by the dreary conventions which tyrannized more fortunate members of society (i.e. the writers and, although trapped in a cruel environment of mean streets and tenements, by a curious inversion he also emerged as the ultimate victor. He escaped emasculation and the bounded existential possibilities which middle-class life offered. Immaculate in poverty, he lived out the blocked options of a generation of white radical intellectuals (47)

On the Road presents this familiar Black culture mentioned by Hebdige "... the hipster and beat subcultures grew out of the same basic mythology, the two styles drew on black culture in different ways and were positioned differently in relation to that culture ... the hipster style was assembled in relatively close proximity to the ghetto black" (47) and Jack Kerouac uses black subculture for identity construction. Subcultures are crucial to the formation of identity outside of class boundaries and in subcultures gender is overlooked. The concern is mainly the solution of problems of young men and girls are invisible and this is also true for black cultures. Youth culture is deeply concerned with the issues of masculinity (Brake 163). Therefore, Sal is in love with Terry, the Mexican girl, to experience Mexican culture.

On the Road is also significant in its depiction of femininity and women in their relation to particularly Dean at a time when there was a tendency to label women and girls bad/mad or hysterical/ lesbian. Therefore, the novel *On the Road,* also alludes to the development of psychiatric institutions and mental health care and hygiene as there were cross-national inquiries by doctors and others who were curious to learn about psychiatry in other parts of the Western world, who wanted to find a model to adopt in their home countries after having taken their international study trips (Gijswijt-Hofstra et al. 9). Besides the various conferences about the state of mental health, the World Health Organization played an active part in generating information in various countries in order to set international standards for it (9). Likewise, Kerouac investigates the role of psychiatry on mental health in America by portraying the dependent and addictive relationship between based on alcohol, drugs, girls and of Dean, Sal and the gang members. A comparative psychiatric culture between America and Europe is difficult to outlay scientifically. Historians of psychiatry were less concerned in the comparative approach of psychiatry as their focus were their home countries mainly (9) reflecting this fact the condition of the mental health of the American Nation as 'a superpower and world savior' after WWI and WWII, is the focal point in *On The Road.* Furthermore, there is confusion with concepts and terms in the studies done in 19th and in 20th century and they do not present a systematic and fully fledged comparative research:

> The term 'mental health care', for example, does not have the same meaning in various national cultures. In some, it refers to a wide sphere of activity, including the care for the mentally handicapped and demented elderly as well as outpatient facilities and counseling centres for psychological and social problems. In others, it mainly concerns psychiatry in a narrower sense: the care and treatment of the mentally ill.

> The way the boundaries of the mental health domain were and are drawn as well as its relation to adjacent fields, such as poor relief, general health care, social work, pastoral care, education, and justice, vary from nation to nation. Concepts like 'social psychiatry', 'psychotherapy', and 'de-institutionalisation' may give rise to confusion. In some countries, psychotherapy and counseling were part and parcel of psychiatry and (public) mental health care, but in others they developed in the context of private practice, psychosomatic medicine, or social work. (10)

In the twentieth century, people relied on popular scientific knowledge and there was the use of regularized expert knowledge, about personal and social life as a constitutive element in its organization and transformation (Gijswijt-Hofstra et al. 15). Until far into the twentieth century, institutional psychiatry fulfilled two functions medical (cure and care) and sociopolitical (segregation). After 1950 the "medical care model" was rejected setting a new moral agenda and de-institutionalization began (17). There was also the introduction of new psychotropic drugs, referred to as the 'psychopharmacological revolution' (17). There was a conflict between psychoanalysis and its applications on people, which did not seem to offer much help for the labeled (bad, mad, homosexual and abnormal) individuals and anti-psychiatric movement paved its way amidst the confusion regarding the psychiatric culture and the intellectual background of America. The opposing views of behaviorism and psychoanalysis shaped the American way of thinking. Direct application of scientific methods and findings on human beings for the betterment of human life was the only concern. The conflict between them caused a split in modern thought. The psychoanalysts believed that insight preceded and accompanied freedom and the behaviorists believed that freedom and liberating insights are illusions and habit formed by conditioning is the basis of human life and happiness in society and individual life. Both schools therapeutic and religious were concerned with the cure of human dysfunctions and the sickness of the mind and the soul. Behaviorism wanted to modify behavior by external influence and psychoanalysis looked for the source of one's illness and the key to one's cure in the individual (Hoffman 19).

The focus was on the creation of the consumerist middleclass "Little Man," who was white, male and normal. After 1920, Freud's theories sparked a "sexual reformation," and with Kinsey's justifications, "sex" was no longer seen as a feeling but as an action. Sex was more of a "release" or "outlet" that involved physical exertion. The opposing views of behaviorism and psychoanalysis shaping American thought split modern thought. The creation of identity, which resulted in fixation, addiction, and fragmentation, was influenced by learning theories Kinsey (1948) built his theories on the discovery upon unhappy effects (neurosis and psychosis) of civilization's repression of sexual instinct. In doing this, his aim was to help patients free themselves from the ignorance of sex fostered by his bourgeois morality. The repression of the sexual desire, on the other hand, was essential for civilization and the achievements of culture so far that sexual energy could be rechanneled into art, religion and thought (Hoffman 23). Kinsey did not describe homosexuality as sickness; it was just a hidden fact experienced by one-third of the male population in society (Hoffman 24). Despite these views that dominated the intellectual scene, the police and the government committed crimes against those who were "different"; homosexuals and communists.

Kerouac's travels with his companion Neil Cassady are mirrored as fictitious in the book amid this cerebral strife; travel is a metaphor for mobility and American democracy. The interaction between Sal Paradise and wild crazy Dean Moriarty, the New American Saint, illustrates how challenging it is to forge a meaningful self-identity based on an authentic self in a society that values sameness and consumption; Sal Paradise, sitting by the bank of a river, reflecting on the American landscapes he has seen on his travels, still thinking of mad Dean Moriarty at the end of the novel. He is haunted by the ideas of Dean Moriarty, as suggested by the pun and irony on his surname; morality, theology, and belief, and, also being a geographical place, Moriarty is a city in Torrance County, Albuquerque, New Mexico, an annexed land from Mexico. Kerouac has created his alternative Saint to criticize religion and ideology to be scientifically studied as a cause for madness, youth and societal problems. Madness was a fact of America and religion played a great role both in inducing madness and dealing with madness at the same time.

Madness and Dean Moriarty (Theology)

Theological beliefs and practical considerations shaped responses to madness and churchgoers wondered why mental illness existed and how it should be responded. In America right from the beginning:

> They accepted sickness as part of what it meant to be human and finite. Under continual debate was whether mental illness was a physical, spiritual, social, or moral problem, or some combination thereof. Believers pointed to sin—original or personal, corporate or individual—as the culprit of all illness, including mental disorders. A few even insisted on direct links between individual behavior and mental maladies.

> Suspicions of demonic possession and illness as divine punishment appeared, but, in America, those explanations diminished as the centuries progressed. (Vacek 160)

Individual and social failures were viewed as the cause of insanity. Personal culpability resulted in permanent illness. Women and men who refused to give up willful wrongdoing, moral laxity, and deviant behavior contributed to the continuation of illness (160). Homosexuality and masturbation were considered deviant behavior. Churchgoers also blamed secular and ecclesial institutions for treating those who were labelled ill (homosexual). On the other hand, madness became a part of many people's life posing important problems for the family members and "diagnosis and treatment" became a regular habit without expertise:

> An increasingly complex society made mental distress inevitable, especially for populations deemed vulnerable to illness, including minorities, immigrants, the poor, and women. American Protestants diagnosed individuals, society, and sometimes both as sick and in need of treatment. Churchgoers explored the proper location and method of treatment. Healing efforts emerged in congregations and church-sponsored facilities, but Protestants also affirmed a role for state-run and private institutions, particularly for more acute cases. Confession of sinful behavior and intercessory prayers offered on behalf of sufferers supplemented medical care. Preventative measures, like early twentieth-century mental hygiene initiatives, also attracted Protestant attention. Regardless of treatment locations or approaches, Christians hoped to bring relief from suffering and enable cures. Believers professed confidence in both human and divine agency in healing, although inclinations about who should lead caregiving efforts differed. Spiritual care seemed within the purview of clergy, but laity, asserting their place in the priesthood of all believers, identified ways to help. Serving at hospitals as chaplains, mental health professionals, and volunteer caregivers fulfilled a sense of Christian duty. Alongside lay involvement, both clergy and physicians claimed authority in the diagnosis and care of mental distress, but the formalization of scientific medical care brought tensions. (161)

There was a strong cooperation between religious (mainly Protestants) and medical professionals (161). As the central concern was related to healing and they relied on Jesus's example and command (161). Fear and stigma dominated the scene. Suffering and mental illness were going in hand in hand. Stifling depression, crippling anxiety, and frightening delusions were undesired symptoms. Medical attention helped to reduce symptoms but formal diagnoses like chronic depression, obsessive-compulsive disorder, or schizoaffective disorder, etc. remained permanent though diagnoses were reductive they were not helpful, as pharmaceuticals relieved symptoms, but had unpleasant side effects. And diagnostic labeling; "a schizophrenic," "a manic depressive," or "crazy" itself is a cause for further distress and suffering. (161)

Namely, severe mental distress means existential difficulties, and for Christians, it has theological reflection (162). On the other hand, madness is a reality in the contemporary world and, therefore, must be understood. The anti-psychiatrist Roland D. Laing describes madness (1967) as liberation from restraints. It is a renewal and an existential death. When a person goes mad his center of experience moves from ego to self. Mundane time becomes anectodal, and only the eternal matters. And the madman becomes confused and muddles ego with self, inner and outer, natural and supernatural, and loses his sense of self and feelings and his place in the world we know and tells us he is dead. Since his visions and voices seem senseless to us: we want to cleanse and cure him (133). For Laing, madness is not an illness to cure. Crime is the natural outcome in a society committed by respectable men, doctors, lawyers, teachers, family members, and the police. The experience of Remi and Sal as cops is remarkable with whom Sal comes to witnesses police crime; only Remi and his laugh roaring over the California woods and America (Kerouac 72), enables Sal to endure the job for a short period of time. Although he has several mad schemes about revenge in his mind (68) and is in a constant battle with the system, he is entrapped in the same phrase of President Truman and in the vicious crime cycle as everybody else:

> "You know what President Truman said?" She was delighted. I suddenly began to realize that everybody in America is a natural-born thief. I was getting the bug myself. I even began to try to see if doors were locked. The other cops were getting suspicious of us; they saw it in our eyes; they understood with unfailing instinct what was in our minds. Years of experience had taught them the likes of Remi and me. (71)

The family in another crucial concept playing its role in the preservation and continuation of the dominant culture as defined by Laing (1967):

> The family's function is to repress Eros; to induce a false consciousness of security; to deny death by avoiding life; to cut of transcendence; to believe in God, not to experience the Void; to create, in short, one-dimensional man; to promote respect, conformity, obedience; to con

children out of play; to induce a fear of failure; to promote a respect for work; to promote a respect for respectability." (65)

Therefore the family as an institution is absent in the novel and there are aunts like in tribal communities supporting the growth of girls and boys into adulthood. Sal and other gang members are supported by their aunts financially and the father and mother figures are absent to break the function of the economic metaphor another concept of Laing (1967):

> The economic metaphor is aptly employed. The mother "invests" in her child. What is most revealing is the husband's function, the provision of economic support, status and protection, in that order. There is frequent reference to security, the esteem of others. What one is supposed to want, to live for, is "gaining pleasure from the esteem and affection of others"[8] if not, one is a psychopath. Such statements are in a sense true. They describe the frightened, cowed, abject creature that we are admonished to be, if we are to be normal offering each other mutual protection from our own violence, the family as a "protection racket." (63-64)

The gang members can break free from all the restraints, like the black man playing Jazz and blowing free, but becoming abject and abnormal. Dean, although very well acquainted with Carlo and an inspiration for the gang members, is not aware of himself and needs to construct an authentic identity via writing:

> In the bar I told Dean, "Hell, man, I know very well you didn't come to me to want to become a writer, and after all what do I really know about it except you've got to stick to it with the energy of benny addict." And he said, "Yes, of course, I know exactly what you mean and in fact all those problems have occurred to me, but the thing that I want is the realization of those factors that should one depend on Schopenhaur's dichotomy for any inwardly realized ..."and so on in that way, things I understood not a bit and he himself didn't. In those days he really didn't know what he was talking about; that is to say, he was a young jailkid all hung-upon the wonderful possibilities of becoming a real intellectual ... he wasn't so naïve as that in all other things, and it took him just a few months with Carlo Marx to become completely *in there* with all the terms and jargons. (Kerouac 6)

The Beat Generation is the slogan or label for a revolution in manners in America. Kerouac viewed Beat philosophy and culture as a way of living (Womack 20). On the contrary, the Beat philosophy and culture were widely misinterpreted in the popular media in 1957 and later 1958. The term Beat was associated with juvenile delinquency by everybody, press and TV and Hollywood began to call that Beat, that beatific ... (42, 79)" as cited in Womack (20) when Kerouac gets full of rage on those stigmatized with crime and don't understand the dark 'criminal history of America' (my emphasis):

> ...woe unto those who don't realize that America must, will, is, changing now, for the better I say. Woe unto those who believe in the atom bomb, who believe in hating mothers and fathers, who deny the most important of the Ten Commandments, woe unto those (though) who don't believe in the unbelievable sweetness of sex love, woe unto those who are the standard bearers of death, woe unto those who believe in conflict and horror and violence and fill our books and screens and living rooms with all that crap, woe in fact unto those who make evil movies about the Beat Generation where innocent housewives are raped by beatniks! (Kerouac 79)

Kerouac achieved his revolutionary goal of opening a space for a new spirituality with his depiction of mobility, traveling, and being on the Road, a mobility synonymous with a search for an American essence. Haunted by the spirit of the outlaw, the hobo, and the pioneer, Kerouac juxtaposes the images of settlers, farmers, townspeople, and the cowboy (Cresswell 261) and decenters them. His zigzagging plot matches the zigzagging language, though Kerouac uses standard grammar and chapters upon request of the editor. *On the Road* was written as a 120-foot-long continuous unpunctuated paragraph on the role of teletype in six days (256). Kerouac attempted to create a nonstop statement of experience to break through conventional forms of writing and thereby produce the necessary energy for change, as evident in the edited version of the book. The sentences reflect the blowing and breathing of a saxophone solo called (by Kerouac) Spontaneous Bop Prosody, acknowledging the influence of jazz (Creswell 256). Echoing the creation of the world in six days, he by destroying the pre-established forms of Self, Identity, the Language and all forms of writing and creates the world anew.

Conclusion

On the Road is about counter writing, a revolutionary act. Kerouac, via travel writing and pilgrimage-like experiential journey, observes and analyzes the deluded Dean Moriarty and himself, reflecting the relationship between the American Dream and America. After Dean leaves Sal in his delusionary state to go to Inez, Sal realizes Dean is a member of the rat race, but at the same time, he also understands the impossible complexity of his life, as he has to get on with his wives and woes (Kerouac 393). Dean is torn between his three (awakening) wives alluding to the difficulty of change and protofeminism and runs away from responsibility: Camille is the helper to the priest, Marylou, the sexy, independent, and attractive one, and Inez, a Mexican nun, and poet called Sor Juana Inés de la Cruz (1648–1695), who was the forerunner of the women's independence and championed women's rights through her writing and "demonstrates the opportunities available to nuns who lived within the supportive same-sex community that is the convent" at court (Sierra 207). Jack Kerouac tries to overcome the mutability of the impossible dream by writing about his experiences (as a writer) and the plight of the subcultures (of writers) in the parent/dominant culture, ironically represented by Dean Moriarty and those who admire him. Moriarty is the new Saint to decenter god, race, ideology, ethnicity, and gender-centered viewpoint of the capitalistic American society, to make the basic foundations of the American Nation; be put in question as well as his attempt at a reconstruction of America. The roots of Moriarty go back to Ireland and a town in New Mexico, like the background of immigrant Sal Paradise (Jack Kerouac) questioning his own identity in a society with a stereotyping and othering tendency, making the readers aware of the original inhabitants' cultures and their problems by presenting an intellectual counter-culture by writing. The Subcultures are multiple, and an individual group member may enter one subculture or several subcultures (Dowd and Dowd 21) at one or another. Sal and the gang members learn, as announced by Kerouac, the Earth is an Indian thing, and Mexico gives "the opportunity to learn ourselves" (Tytell 88) near the end of *On the Road.* In their cyclic travels and completion of the initiation into society, "the rite de passage is complete" after having investigated the mental and geographical (health) spaces after reconquering and contaminating all contested places of America through the inner and outer voyages done by a subcultural group of young writers, the Beats.

Bibliography

Berger, Bennett M. “How Long Is a Generation?” The British Journal of Sociology, vol. 11, no. 1, 1960, pp. 10–23. JSTOR, https://doi.org/10.2307/587038. Accessed 18 Jul. 2022.

Britannica, The Editors of Encyclopedia. "Beat movement". Encyclopedia Britannica, 24 Mar. 2021, https://www.britannica.com/art/Beat-movement. Accessed 22 July 2022.

Creighton, Joanne V. *Joyce Carol Oates: Novels of the Middle Years*. New York: Twayne Publishers, 1992.

Cresswell, Tim. “Mobility as Resistance: A Geographical Reading of Kerouac’s ‘On the Road.’” Transactions of the Institute of British Geographers, vol. 18, no. 2, 1993, pp. 249–62. JSTOR, https://doi.org/10.2307/622366. Accessed 18 Jul. 2022.

Devienne, Elsa. “The Life, Death, and Rebirth of Muscle Beach: Reassessing the Muscular Physique in Postwar America, 1940s–1980s.” Southern California Quarterly, vol. 100, no. 3, 2018, pp. 324–67. JSTOR, https://www.jstor.org/stable/26499889. Accessed 18 Jul. 2022.

Dowd, James J., and Laura A. Dowd. “The Center Holds: From Subcultures to Social Worlds.” *Teaching Sociology*, vol. 31, no. 1, 2003, pp. 20–37. JSTOR, https://doi.org/10.2307/3211422. Accessed 18 Jul. 2022.

Johnson, Joyce, 1935-. The Voice Is All: The Lonely Victory of Jack Kerouac. [Jack Kerouac'ın Yalnız Yaşamı: Anlatım herşeydir]. Trans. Aydın Çavdar, İstanbul: Ayrıntı Yayınları, 2017. (Originally Published 2012)

Johnston, Allan. “Consumption, Addiction, Vision, Energy: Political Economies and Utopian Visions in the Writings of the Beat Generation.” College Literature, vol. 32, no. 2, 2005, pp. 103–26. JSTOR, http://www.jstor.org/stable/25115269. Accessed 18 Jul. 2022.

Hebdige, Dick. Subculture: The meaning of style. Routledge, 2012.

Holmes, J.C..“ This Is the Beat Generation.” The New York Times Magazine, 1952, 16 November, pp. 10, 19–20, 22. In Levi Asher “This Is The Beat Generation” by John Clellon Holmes, 1994, July 24, “This Is The Beat Generation” by John Clellon Holmes. https://litkicks.com/thisisthebeatgeneration/

Hoffman, Daniel, and Braudy, Leo, editors. *Harvard Guide to Contemporary American Writing.* Cambridge Mass: Bellknapp Press of Harvard University Press, 1979.

Kazin, M., Edwards, R., & Rothman, A. editors. *The Concise Princeton Encyclopedia of American Political History.* Princeton University Press, 2011.

Kerouac, Jack. *On the Road.* The Viking Press, 1957.

Laing, Ronald. D. *The Politics of Experience*. New York: Pantheon, 1967.

Malcolm, Douglas. "'Jazz America': Jazz and African American Culture in Jack Kerouac's 'On the Road.'" *Contemporary Literature*, vol. 40, no. 1, 1999, pp. 85–110. JSTOR, https://doi.org/10.2307/1208820. Accessed 18 Jul. 2022.

Mcgeachan, Cheryl. 'The World is full of Big Bad wolves': Investigating the Experimental Therapeutic Spaces of R.D. Laing and Aaron Esterson. *History of Psychiatry* 25, 283–298, 2014. https://doi:10.1177/0957154x14529222

Prothero, Stephen. "On the Holy Road: The Beat Movement as Spiritual Protest." The Harvard *Theological Review*, vol. 84, no. 2, 1991, pp. 205–22. JSTOR, http://www.jstor.org/stable/1509800. Accessed 18 Jul. 2022.

A Companion to American Literature, edited by Susan Belasco, et al., John Wiley & Sons, Incorporated, 2020. ProQuest Ebook Central, http://ebookcentral.proquest.com/lib/anadolu/detail.action?docID=6157421. Created from anadolu on 2022-07-20 15:25:32.

Psychiatric Cultures Compared: *Psychiatry and Mental Health Care in the Twentieth Century - Comparisons and Approaches*, edited by Marijke Gijswijt-Hofstra, et al., Amsterdam University Press, 2005. ProQuest Ebook Central, http://ebookcentral.proquest.com/lib/anadolu/detail.action?docID=420238. Created from anadolu on 2022-07-20 14:50:05.

Roberts, Robert E., and Cornelius, Askew, Jr. "A Consideration of Mortality in Three Subcultures." *Health Services Reports*, vol. 87, no. 3, 1972, pp. 262–70. JSTOR, https: //doi.org/10.2307/4594487.Accessed 18 Jul. 2022.

Sierra, Horacio. "Gossiping Women and Talkative Nuns:The Transatlantic Feminism of María de Zayas and Sor Juana Inés de la Cruz." *Women's Studies*, vol.50, no.3, 202, pp. 207-223,

DOI: 10.1080/00497878.2020.1855180

Tytell, John. *Writing Beat and Other Occasions of Literary Mayhem*, Vanderbilt University Press, 2014. ProQuest Ebook Central, https://offcampus.anadolu.edu.tr:2364/lib/anadolu/detail.action?docID=3040168.

Womack, Steven. "Popular Media Representations of Beat Culture; or, Jack Kerouac Meets Maynard G. Krebs." *Studies in Popular Culture*, vol. 24, no. 3, 2002, pp. 17–24. JSTOR, http://www.jstor.org/stable/23414963. Accessed 18 Jul. 2022.

Vacek, Heather H. *Madness: American Protestant Responses to Mental Illness*, Baylor University Press, 2015. ProQuest Ebook Central, http://ebookcentral.proquest.com/lib/anadolu/detail.action?docID=2100951.

A Short Bio of Assist. Prof. Dr. Dilek Ünügür ÇALIŞKAN:

Dilek Ünügür Çalışkan is an Assistant Professor at Anadolu University and teaches literature classes. She studies the relationships between the Self and the "Other:" in sociological, psychological, environmental, and cultural contexts, as well as, Identity types and their construction; Queer Identities, Gender Identity, Hybridity (hum-animals), and Eco-self in the context of madness (schizophrenia and schizoanalysis, Mythology/Shamanism and Eco-sophy).

The Subversion of The Traditional Image of The Explorer-Hero in Eric Newby's *Round Ireland in Low Gear* (1987)

Res. Assist. Dr. Elif DEMİR

Abstract

Eric Newby in *Round Ireland in Low Gear* (1987) travels to Ireland with his wife Wanda. Their account subverts the traditional image of the explorer-hero in specific ways: The cult of the explorer-hero is based on a national ambition, yet Eric and Wanda travel for amusement. Besides, women are historically excluded from travel accounts as they are viewed as lacking strength, yet Eric travels with his wife. The instances of weakness and failure are presented during their travel although a traditional explorer is a strong figure. Instead of emphasizing courage, they do not take their actions seriously. Although the traditional image is brave to conquer unknown territories, Eric and Wanda lack the prowess and prove to be anti-heroes in their journey. Textually, humorous and self-ironizing attitudes subvert the conventional understanding of heroism. Therefore, this study aims to examine how the traditional figure of the explorer-hero is challenged in the selected work.

Keywords: Traditional travel writing, Explorer-hero, Subversion, Eric and Wanda, *Round Ireland in Low Gear*

Introduction

Despite having a long history in the literary tradition, the genre of travel writing is brought to the academic agenda in a new dimension after Edward Said's *Orientalism* (1978) which presents the borders of the self and other in the dichotomy of the West and East. Although there are post-war travel accounts dealing with travelling to the eastern countries in the same orientalist vein of Said, there are also works which depict the experiences about travelling to the West. As one of them, Eric Newby, who is a well-known British travel writer, travels to Ireland with his wife Wanda in his work entitled *Round Ireland in Low Gear* (1987). His travel accounts include places across the world ranging from India to Italy, from Afghanistan to Russia. Among the British travel writers of post-war era (such as Dervla Murphy, Norman Lewis, Jan Morris, Colin Thubron, and Patrick Leigh Fermor), Eric Newby gains a place in the genre through his ironical and comic mode of representation which can also be observed in the selected work.

Eric Newby cannot simply be called a traveller, yet he is an explorer. Robin Hanbury-Tenison argues that explorers differ from travellers in the sense that they are "driven by a desire to discover which transcends the urge to conquer, the pursuit of trade, the curiosity of the scientist, the zeal of the missionary, or the simple search for adventure" (x). As an explorer, Eric Newby suggests in the "Introduction" of *A Traveller's Life* (1982) that he travels "for amusement and sheer curiosity" (3), which nourishes his desire to search for adventure. Evelyn Waugh in the preface of Newby's second work *A Short Walk in the Hindu Kush* (1958) states that "It was the longing, romantic, reasonless, which lies deep in the hearts of most Englishmen, to shun the celebrated spectacles of the tourist and without any concern with science or politics or commerce, simply to set their feet where few civilized feet have trod" (11-12). Therefore, Newby is an explorer driven by his curiosity rather than bearing scientific or financial goals. Likewise, in the "Introduction" of the selected work, he explains his intention to travel to Ireland as follows: "We were not going to travel in the guise of sociologists, journalists or contemporary historians" (*Round* ix), but "We were going there, in short, to enjoy ourselves, an unfashionable aspiration in the 1980s" (*Round* x). Hence, Newby is a modern explorer-hero who leaves behind the scientific and commercial concerns of his antecedents but travels for enjoyment and adventure.

Along with the purpose of travel, the means of transportation is quite essential for Eric Newby who clarifies in his works why he chose that specific vehicle for the journey. In *A Short Walk in the Hindu Kush* (1958), he complains that "If there is any way of seeing less of a country than from a motor car I have yet to experience it" (63-64). Because he expects a vehicle to enable him to see around better, he also discusses the means of transportation to be employed in *Round Ireland in Low Gear* (1987). Although his first impulse is to walk it, he later thinks that it is a time-consuming way because his plans cover to see there between December and March. Even though the weather conditions are harsh in the wintertime, he chooses to pedal along the country because employing a car keeps one focused on the road and the other focused on map-reading rather than giving chance to appreciate the scenes. He believes that he can only persuade his wife Wanda to use a bicycle; however, Wanda accepts to travel with him because "If I [she] come it will only be to make sure you [he] don't get into trouble" (*Round* 11).

On such a challenging journey, Eric and Wanda explore as much as they can. However, they fall outside of the characteristics of being a conventional explorer-hero. The text subverts the traditional image of the explorer-hero in specific ways: Firstly, the cult of the explorer-hero is based on a "manly" image of a macho persona; however, the instances of weakness and failure are presented during their travel. For example, they are almost run over by trucks and trailers, they are frequently rain-soaked, and a dog bites Eric's ankle. Although the manly figure withstands difficulties and completes the quest successfully, Eric and Wanda stop if it is impossible to pedal more. Even, they return to England from time to time. Concerning this, women are historically excluded from travel accounts as they are viewed as lacking strength, yet Eric travels with his wife Wanda. Both resist the harsh geographic and atmospheric conditions of Ireland despite their advanced age. Although biking is not the easiest way because it requires physical strength, Eric and Wanda pedal for miles in the harsh weather of December. Neither their age nor Wanda's being a woman becomes an obstacle to travel. Besides, comic and self-ironizing attitude subvert the conventional understanding of heroism. Humour begins from the start when he considers which means of transportation is better for their travel. For example, after he explains why a car, motorcycle, train, or bus is not suitable for them, he also receives horses and balloons for his consideration. As for self-irony, it surfaces in the instances of failure. Although the traditional explorer-hero is courageous to conquer the unknown territories thereby being self-sacrificing and moral, Eric and Wanda lack the prowess and prove to be anti-heroes in their journey. In an instance, Eric warns Wanda to cycle in the correct gear, yet, she rebels that she can no longer bike because she is not a superwoman (*Round* 140). By doing so, she becomes a representative of common sense.

Therefore, she also subverts the traditional gender constructs subordinating women, which indicates that the subversion in the text is multi-layered. Therefore, this study aims to examine how the traditional understanding of an explorer-hero is challenged in Eric and Wanda's travel to Ireland in the selected work.

The Subversion of The Traditional Explorer-Hero: Eric and Wanda in Ireland

The figure of the explorer originates from a long tradition in the history of England due to the expansionist politics of the country. Because the explorers satisfy the territorial aims of the country, "the explorer has also been fêted as a national hero in whose hands lay the destiny of his country" (Smethurst 366). The national identity nourishes patriotic values by also producing a sense of heroism. Having such a status, however, overshadows the writing process of the exploration, which can be quoted in Sherman's words, "The great explorers were not always interested in writing" (25). He goes on to say that "Walter Raleigh was perhaps the first great explorer to play a significant role in creating his own persona in print. What distinguishes his *Discovery of the Large, Rich, and Beautiful Empire of Guiana* (1595) is both its unprecedented attention to geographic and ethnographic detail and its autobiographical strategies" (Sherman 26). As one of the explorers serving his country's ambitions, Raleigh also writes about his experiences, which is a way to identify Englishness for others. However, Eric Newby does not pursue a national goal in his travel to Ireland. Therefore, his travel is not for exploring the English identity and the other, but rather for the enthusiasm he has for exploring and enjoying a new place. It also functions as a venture to explore his personal limits.

Eric and Wanda travel to Ireland simply to enjoy and appreciate the scenery. In this sense, they differ from the traditional image of the explorer hero who privileges the national, commercial, and territorial ambitions of his country. Eric and Wanda find beauty in what they see whether it is a house in the woods or just a mountain. For instance, when they visited Slieve Bearnagh hills, they are astonished to see a house. Eric describes it as follows: "The entrance front was entirely faced with this silvery stone, and with what was to be the last of a pale, wintry afternoon sun illuminating the windows the house was an enchanting sight. It could have been the abode of some sleeping princess, waiting to be awakened after asleep of centuries" (*Round* 31). For another example, he is astonished at the scenery: "I pedalled on for another four or five miles through the bare limestone plain, the only visible living things in it now blackbirds and rooks. The last of the sun on this beautiful day was shining on the high, treeless tops of the Burren mountains, so convincingly sculpted by nature into the forms of prehistoric camps and forts that it was difficult to know whether I was looking at the work of nature or of man" (*Round* 58). An explorer has the zeal of setting foot on unknown lands. From his description, it can be detected that he is in an awe to see something new which has not been offered to him before in any other countries he has visited. Therefore, it is not a conventional exploration of new territory, but a personal exploration of seeing what is unknown to him. For this reason, he enjoys his travel as he sees either man-constructed or natural scenery even though it costs him to pedal miles and miles. Although the traditional explorers focus on the explored land in terms of its wealth to be benefitted from. Eric succeeds to capture beautiful sceneries and appreciates them. Enjoying the view can easily turn the traveller status into a tourist, but the two terms differ from each other: "while the term 'traveller' offers a positive and independent model of selfhood, 'tourists are never ourselves, always other people'" (Thubron 58). In this sense, Eric and Wanda are travellers, not tourists, as they are "adventurous, spontaneous, genuine, active, curious, and in search of a real and authentic experience of other places and cultures" (Kinsley 382). Because tourists are a part of a group and mainly visit famous hallmarks, the term has negative connotations. Eric and Wanda, however, search for the native compound, spontaneity, and adventure of biking. For this reason, they are not on a limitedly arranged time schedule like tourists, yet, they take their time to explore the details. Eric even says that "We were still only nine miles from Limerick. If we went on like this and I continued to record what I saw in such superfluous detail it would take us five years to travel round Ireland, and the rest of my life to write about it" (34). Because they enjoy the details, it slows their travel pace. Although he is an experienced traveller, he fails to organize how much time it is better to spend at each spot. This stems from the desire to explore and record everything he sees to guarantee that he does not miss to convey his observations. In this regard, he disrupts the traditional explorer figure who seeks to achieve universally accepted territorial supremacy for his country. The conventional figure aims "to establish a certain English reputation" (Das 79); however, Eric Newby more often incorporates subjectivity in his writing as a way of expressing his personal experiences.

Being more subjective arises from financial reasons. Eric and Wanda pay for the expenses of the travel and, therefore, feel freer when penning all sorts of experiences without censorship. However, in traditional exploration writing, "it is important to recognize that explorers were usually actors in collaborative ventures. They relied on patrons, sponsors, collectors, publishers, and governments with global interests, while the geopolitical reality of empire was necessary to their mobility" (Smethurst 367). Because a traditional explorer is sponsored by a person or institution and, therefore, is under an obligation towards the dependant, the accounts turn out to be "promised textual report(s)" (Das 90). Eric begins to write the work from the shopping scenes. They buy new bicycles and all the necessary protective equipment with optional and non-optional extras. After the delivery of bikes, they talk:

> 'We can put it all down to expenses,' I said to Wanda.
>
> 'I wouldn't count on it,' she said. 'I can just see the expression on the Inspector of Taxes' face. He'll laugh all the way to your funeral.'
>
> 'Well, why did you let me buy all this stuff if that's what you think.' I asked.
>
> 'I was going to stop you,' she said, 'but when I saw how much you were enjoying yourself, somehow I couldn't. You looked like a small boy in a sweet shop.' (*Round* 16).

Although she guesses that they buy a lot more than they need, she does not tell it after she sees his enthusiasm and joy. It may cost more but self-sponsoring the travel emancipates the language. Instead of a framed one, Eric is advantageous to fashion his narration without sacrificing his own writing style. He adopts a comic and ironic tone which cannot be observed in traditional travel writings. His having more textual authority enables him to reveal and write the self. Therefore, financial dependency censors the language and sets boundaries in the context.

The text subverts the traditional travel accounts also with the figure of a woman travelling because "It is not a blind spot to define the explorer as male" (Smethurst 367). Wanda is not only a companion while en route, but also, she challenges the traditional image of a traveller in the sense that women are attributed to domestic spaces and therefore, are intentionally excluded from the genre. This taboo takes its source from the traditional gender roles which ascribe mobility to men and immobility to women. Thompson argues that

> in many societies, in many periods, restlessness, freedom of movement and a taste for adventure have been attributes and activities conventionally associated with men rather than women. According to the patriarchal ideology of separate spheres, a woman's proper and preferred location is the home, and women have therefore traditionally been associated with

immobility or, as it is sometimes dubbed 'sessility', and with domesticity (168-169).

Gendering the travel narratives is associated with patriarchy, which hierarchizes the spheres and traps women in the matrix. Because the figure of a woman who nurses her husband and children, run errands, and cares for all domestic issues is idealised, women are deliberately represented with interiority. This traditional image is subverted in Eric Newby's narratives who travel with his wife wherever he explores. At the beginning of the work, Eric is concerned with persuading Wanda to travel to Ireland during such a harsh time of the year, yet he does not think about leaving Wanda behind. Likewise, Wanda seems reluctant but accepts to travel to keep him away from troubles. Wanda not only accompanies him but also supports his author role: "If you skip all the time,' she said severely, 'you will not be able to write your book about Ireland." (*Round* 112). Therefore, Wanda breaks the routine of an immobile woman figure. However, gender roles keep on operating from time to time; for example, it is when they could not find a restaurant open: "So we went to the supermarket and Wanda bought the ingredients of a dinner which, if necessary and providing the stove was still going at the farm, she could cook herself" (*Round* 42). Although she breaks the restrictions of spatial boundaries, she cooks -not Eric- when they need to eat. The masculine association of travelling is reversed, yet gender roles could not be negotiated. In this respect, the paradigm of representation emerges, because the author steers the textual representation. Bird suggests that

> travel writing is a privileged locus of self-fashioning for men on condition that they observe the accepted forms of masculinity: asserting facts rather than indulging feelings, announcing heroism rather than admitting cowardice, accumulating heterosexual conquests and eliding homosexual exploration (81).

The writer has the privileged status of self-fashioning and fashioning the other. Wanda is represented in the role of wife (rather than a traveller) in the instance above. The problem of the representation of the women traveller can also be considered within textual politics as the role of domesticity at home is transferred to the text. In this sense, Pickering argues that "Wives change the tenor of books. Good taste and good sense, at least if a writer values peaceful domesticity, influence books in which wives appear" (483). The text becomes a part of domesticity to be appreciated by the reader. When fashioning the other in terms of the construction of textual identities, the role attributed to the co-traveller, therefore, is also for textual benefits and is in favour of the representer.

Hence, even though travel writing has the power to challenge gender norms, dislocation happens only to a certain extent. As illustrated by Jane Robinson, while travelling "partnership has little to do with equality" (14).

Travelling is also handicapped for women when equipment is concerned. The root of this issue also lies in the historical associations of travel writing. The genre is gendered historically: "The essence of adventure lies in taking risks and exploring the unknown, so it is hardly surprising to find that early travel accounts tended for the most part to be written by men" (Bassnett 225). Because travelling is identified as a male activity, therefore, it is not surprising to observe the exclusion of women in the equipment produced. Eric pens the travel in England from the point where they search for the right bicycles. He states that

> most mountain bike saddles seem to have been designed by men who don't realize that on a mountain bike the rider sits more or less upright, as on a roadster, so that the whole weight of the body, divided on a bicycle with dropped handlebars between the saddle and the bars, falls on the saddle. It is even worse for women. Women have wider hips and, as the *Buyer's Bible* delicately put it, having presumably taken female advice, 'the pubic arch between the legs is shallower, making the genital area very vulnerable to pressure' (*Round* 17).

In their choice of bicycle, they counsel the guidance of the *Buyer's Bible*, which is likely to take a female opinion about the disturbance of saddle. Because women are excluded from adventure, their anatomical differences are also ignored when the structure of a comfortable bicycle is considered. Although men have a wide array of options in choosing a bicycle, women have limited alternatives. Among the bicycles, "Wanda chose a Brooks B72 leather touring saddle, 'specially designed for women cyclists and those wanting a broader support'" (*Round* 18). Travelling and travel writing are historically a restrictive trope for women due to the patriarchal perspective on the subordination of women, but the travel of Wanda to Ireland shows that, from a woman's lenses, little has been changed in terms of regarding travelling as a male domain. For this reason, Wanda, whose Ireland adventure is not her first time, subverts the traditional values of the genre more remarkably since she has more challenges than Eric.

Another feature that enables the subversion of the traditional representation of the explorer figure can be argued within the framework of ageism. A conventional image is also presented as a virile and young man (Bird 81) because he can deal with adversities only with his physical strength. The traditional heroic features are designed to proclaim a ruthless image that fights against constraints. Therefore, virility is another edge of masculine heroism, which is linked with the mobility of men freely in public sphere. Ageing changes the pre-established gender norms, because it is another phase of life in which biological changes operate differently from a young body. Hence, ageing leaves social norms out of gender scope to generate its own cultural dynamics. For example, firstly, as Hyde puts it "Later life has traditionally been thought of as a time of stability, not mobility" (337) and "recently researchers on either side thought older people slowly withdrew from (foreign) travel as they age due, for example, to problems in obtaining travel insurance" (338). Leaving aside the biological changes, ageing in fact is a cultural construct since it is a social norm that attributes stability to ageing. There is a wide variety of reasons for people to withdraw themselves from travelling, which can be listed as poor health, socio-demographic factors, such as education, income and marital status (Hyde 340). It is notable in the work that Eric is sixty-six and Wanda is sixty-three years old when they see Ireland on bikes. Pickering states that "Newby conceived of riding a bicycle around he was sixty-six, an age at which travel writers either store their valises in the attic or retreat into small journeys" (483). Because people are aged by culture, it is an expected cultural construct for an aged person to retreat from society and from all the mobile activities they have done before. Although Eric and Wanda are not figures like, for example Livingstone[1], they travel and enjoy being on the road. Therefore, they subvert the virile figure of the explorer-hero due to their age. In the text, neither Eric nor Wanda hesitates about setting off considering their age as an obstacle. Cycling for long periods of time requires a certain amount of physical strength, but they overcome it. If they need rest, then they stop pedaling. It is only once in the text that Eric regards himself as old: "You've chosen a grand day for it,' an old geezer about the same age as me said as," (*Round* 29). When he sees a man at the same age as he is, he calls him 'old'. However, he does not complain about his age or the difficulty of being on the road at that age. Therefore, even though the above-listed reasons to withdraw from travelling seem obstacles, Eric and Wanda take advantage of, for example, pensioner's cards: "Meanwhile Wanda was buying the tickets at a reduced rate using our international old age pensioners' cards" (*Round* 24). Travelling at a reduced price in England and Ireland supports their budget. Because they are self-sponsored, thinking about expenditures comes before thinking about old age travelling retreat. It is also significant to note that they

---

[1] "Livingstone's reputation as a missionary and explorer was built on accounts of his extraordinary physical feats and resilience. He was mauled by a lion in 1844 and constantly battled a range of diseases and injuries until he succumbed in 1873" (Smethurst 377-378).

spend the last day in England at the home of their daughter who lives in Bristol with her family. Their daughter supports their ambition to travel rather than discouraging them due to their advanced age. Therefore, a supportive atmosphere is already established among family members, which reverses the cultural construct prevailing in society.

An old-aged couple travelling to Ireland subverts the traditional explorer-hero also in the sense that the conventional figure goes on an adventurous quest alone by leaving his family behind. Meens and Sintobin argue that "Scholars generally assumed that, at least until modern times, travel texts had predominantly been written by men because they moved more freely in the public sphere than women, who in these male-gazed narratives thus only functioned as objects of desire or as someone to return home to" (2). Therefore, in classical travel texts family is ostracised and functioned as people who wait for the hero. Even if a woman is included in the travel, she is represented as dependent and in need of protection. This notion is also subversively countered in Eric and Wanda's travel. Companionship is a significant factor in their journey since travelling as a couple has pros and cons. Looking at the positive side, they travel together to support each other in the adversities they encounter. The negative part is due to the conflicts of disagreement, for example, which path to follow, who carries the stuff, where to see etc. Considering the negative side first, the moments of disagreements are quite normal for people travelling together because each side has different perspectives on travelling. For example, Eric prefers to read a map, yet, Wanda likes to ask for directions from local people: "Wanda, one of whose foibles is to have no faith in maps, however good, or map readers, however accomplished, had knocked on a cottage door to inquire the way to Sixmilebridge, for which we were bound and to which I already knew the route" (*Round* 34). Even though Eric already knows the correct direction, Wanda asks a local lady who misguided them. The misinformation given by the old lady takes them to another spot, but Wanda still does not have faith in maps, which causes them to waste time in finding the right path. Another problem can be thought of as carrying the stuff. Although traditionally women seem dependent, on their travel paradoxically Eric is dependent. He takes a lot of necessary and unnecessary things to be carried:

> 'The trouble with you is,' she said, relapsing into her argot, 'you always take too bloddy much. What I had weighed half of that, *and* I had a litre of whisky for you and a litre of wine for me, and that weighed God knows how much.'

> 'All right, Mrs Know-All!' I said, not for the first time. 'Next time *you* carry the tools and spares.'
>
> 'That's not fair,' she said. 'You know I don't know these things. I don't even know how to change gear,' she added pathetically, making me feel a heel, as per usual. 'And don't shout. Anyway,' she went on, changing the subject adroitly, 'why do you want two pairs of long stockings, two thick shirts and a pair of shoes when you're already wearing stockings, a thick shirt and a pair of boots!'
>
> 'I thought I might get wet,' I said lamely. (*Round* 103-104)

Eric is an experienced traveller; however, he takes many spare clothes, books, and all other things. They travel by bike and take more than a biker can carry. Because mountain bikes are heavier than urban bikes and have more gears, it is not surprising for Wanda to find extras outweighing them. The loads also change the balance of bicycles, which makes them harder to ride. For instance, they had to reload and load their belongings once:

> The only thing to do was to drive them down the Canal embankment using the only weapons we had, our bicycle pumps, unload both bikes completely, then lift them five feet in the air and over the fence, trying to avoid puncturing the tyres on the wire, wishing all the time that we had lightweights instead of mountain bikes weighing in at 38 pounds (*Round* 224).

Wanda is right about their burden because they have difficulty in carrying them when they need to have lighter loads. This leads Eric to confess at the end of the travel that "Now that the whole thing was more or less over I realized that we hadn't really needed mountain bikes at all: there had been no point at which we had required those enormous great tyres, and two chainwheels and twelve gears would have been quite sufficient" (*Round* 298). From Eric's lens, Wanda seems to complain but what she says is justified in the end by Eric. Therefore, Wanda becomes a figure of common sense, an inner voice of the reader. In this respect, Eric needs the support of Wanda to carry all the stuff, therefore, Wanda reverses the prescribed role of a woman who depends on male strength and who is traditionally 'irrational'. The disagreements happen but, in the end, they find a way to cope with. Because they travel together for a long time and have the experience to know the travel habits of each other, the problems of companionship are solved between them.

On the bright side of their companionship lies their support for each other when they face an adversity. The obstacles are an inevitable part of travelling, and in terms of the traditional travel narratives, the explorer-hero encounters many different threats because overcoming them heroizes the explorer. Wanda travels with Eric to keep him away from troubles, but it is an intermittent journey as they suspend it by going back to England from time to time. At such a time when Wanda was not with Eric, he says that "I was by now in fairly good condition after all this biking and I decided to try for the top in an hour again, something Wanda would have forbidden, had she been present" (*Round* 270). Wanda is cautious but Eric is after adventure, which is a feature of the traditional explorers also have. He loses common sense without Wanda and takes risks to fashion his image. Bird states that "Travel writing is a privileged locus of self-fashioning for men on condition that they observe the accepted forms of masculinity: asserting facts rather than indulging feelings, announcing heroism rather than admitting cowardice," (82). A traditional explorer-hero shows his adventurous character more because he associates his identity with courageous and heroic actions which prove his achievement at the end. Because the hero represents his country, he takes heroism for granted. In this sense, Hanbury-Tenison argues that "their achievements and, indeed, their failures have a lasting significance which may affect the destiny of mankind. As a result, they tend to take themselves rather seriously" (x). Because the traditional explorer does not set off on a journey simply for fun, he feels responsible towards his country and especially towards his sponsor. For this reason, heroism becomes a significant feature of the explorer. Even if he encounters a constraint, he overcomes it with his courage. Therefore, he is successful from start to finish. Wanda keeps Eric away from risky routes and she does not have the urge to be successful during the entire journey. She only aims to keep her health in good condition. Thus, she chooses the known paths. However, a journey offers different sorts of surprises to deal with. The weather conditions are the most challenging obstacle as they travel in wintertime. For example, when they were passing through Sarsfield Bridge to head for County Claire, they were almost drowned: "We were pushing our bikes along the footpath, not even riding them, but still being deluged with un-recycled Irish rainwater that was being thrown up by the west-bound trucks whose drivers, deprived of the pleasure of actually 'kilting' us, were now doing their best to drown us, and were damn nearly succeeding" (*Round* 29). They are almost at the beginning of their journey when they encounter their first harsh weather condition. Being on a bike causes one to be driven away compared to other means of transportation. It restricts the vision and makes the bike hard to control. Luckily, they are not blown or drowned in the first obstacle. During their journey, the weather gives them a rough ride. At another time when the weather is even colder "she was now so cold, in spite of her Korean gloves, that she had lost all feeling in her fingers" (*Round* 174), or when the winds are strong:

> I'm afraid I can't go on with much more of this,' said Wanda, as we sat in a deep valley leading down to the sea next door to an abandoned Morris done out in jungle camouflage with nothing inside except seatbelts. 'The winds and the rains are simply killing me.' And she shed a tear or two (*Round* 163).

The weather challenges more than expected but they keep on travelling. Their companionship functions as a supportive one in such instances. Both have hard times, and they go on together. However, the weather is not the only obstacle. For example, they ride through an unlighted road: "I'm frightened, *really* frightened.' And she was right to be. This particular section of the N18 was single carriageway; it was unilluminated, either due to a power failure or because someone had forgotten to switch on the streetlights" (*Round* 43). After a long day when she thinks that she "finally found a spot that seemed to be to her liking she discovered, too late, that it was infested with stinging nettles" (*Round* 134). In another instance, they are almost killed by trucks: "The same thing had happened to Wanda. By screwing my head round I could see the light from her bicycle's headlamp, but I could see and hear nothing else because of the pandemonium on the road and I had a terrible feeling of panic, afraid that she might be either dead or badly injured" (*Round* 44). The inevitable part of travelling is obstacles, yet they do not aim to heroize their actions. They overcome difficulties merely to survive and go on safely. Because their purpose is not to heroize themselves, their achievements or failures do not bear serious meanings. In this regard, they subvert the traditional understanding of heroism in travel writing. Because a traditional explorer-hero exalts his courage as he represents his country and its glory. However, Eric and Wanda do not hesitate to present the instances of failure and do not portray themselves as always successful. They voice it when they have difficulty in reaching a spot. This subversion also contributes to the textual richness because the moments of self-irony do not only show their being anti-heroes in the quest but also challenge the traditional travel narratives which do not include ironic or comic elements.

In terms of self-ironizing attitude, the most remarkable example is when Wanda criticizes the exaggerated physical strength of the traditional explorer-hero through her inadequacy. Wanda is not a professional mountain biker after all. In one instance, she finds it difficult to choose the correct gear to ride. On the one hand, the roads are quite compelling and on the other, they manage to ride with the help of experiences they gained on the road. Eric notices that she is in the wrong gear and warns him to prevent an accident:

> 'This is too much,' she said. 'I'm going to walk.'
>
> 'It's easier riding,' I said. 'You're just in the wrong gear.'
>
> 'I don't care what gear it's in,' she said. 'I'm not a superwoman. You ride, I'm walking.' (*Round* 140).

Wanda's patience runs out since they are on the road for a long time. For this reason, she gets angry when Eric warns him about the gear. Although she could put an effort to find the correct one, she gives up trying. Although the traditional explorer figures do not always show their weakness or failures, Wanda criticizes this stance of portraying the hero as capable all the time. This irony not only contributes to narrative complexity but also reverses the expectation that the explorer-hero is always intrepid or accomplished. In terms of showing the difficulty of travelling, Wanda's reaction offers a hint at the realities of travelling. In this regard, she subverts the image of a mighty explorer-hero. She stops and exclaims that she is not a super woman, therefore, she represents what awaits an explorer on the same route. Thus, Eric and Wanda become anti-heroes with their failures in the exploration.

The other most important textual element that subverts the traditional travel narratives is also the one, which gives Eric Newby his own writing style that separates him from other writers. Newby is an acclaimed writer who is one of the eminent representatives of comic travel writing. The comic elements in the text are not only a subversion of the traditional accounts but also an element shifting narrative seriousness. His sense of humour is presented in different circumstances. For example, when he implies the difficulty of riding a heavy load, he says that "To me it was much as I imagined it would be to ride a heavily loaded camel, the principal difference being that you don't have to pedal a camel" (*Round* 32). Wanda makes fun of the rainwater of the country:

> 'Did you know,' I said to Wanda, trying to be cultural while pretending to admire this desperate, watery scene, 'that the inventor of the submarine was born here?'
>
> 'If the weather was anything like this when he lived here,' she said, 'inventing the submarine was probably the only way he could keep dry.' (*Round* 87).

Even if he wants to seem cultural, Wanda mocks that the only choice for keeping his body dry for the inventor is to invent the submarine. Eric also includes comic husband and wife quarrels, which is also an element that is not available in the conventional texts. They make fun of the appearance of a peasant they see but also Wanda makes fun of how Eric looks:

> A car passed, going in the opposite direction, and the four occupants waved to us cheerily, as did a young man in shirt sleeves, waistcoat and cap who was in a ditch, wielding a fearsome-looking slashing instrument on a long handle that made him look like a survivor of the Peasants' Revolt.
>
> 'It must be your Jackie Hooghly hat,' Wanda said. 'They think we're Americans.' (*Round* 32).

He resembles the worker of a peasant of former times, yet Eric's hat makes him smile. Therefore, it is not one-sided prejudice that is done with pejorative intentions. While Eric explains the purpose of their travel, he says that it is to enjoy themselves. The comic elements function as a tool to show the reader how they enjoy it and at the same time, it arouses humorous amusement in the reader. For this reason, Eric includes comic elements in the narrative not to offend the people, cultural values, or country but he reinforces his writing style. For example, during their travel, they meet many people called O'Sullivan and Eric humorously says: "Recklessly we hired yet another taxi owned by yet another O'Sullivan — in Ireland you can travel for days through regions in which all the inhabitants appear to have the same name" (*Round* 187). When considering the grave attitude of the traditional explorer-hero, Newby produces a comic reversal of this image through narrative techniques. The seriousness is also shattered through the context when Eric and Wanda talk about their dreams or horoscopes. In their dream, Eric invites King George VI to dine with him, and in Wanda's dream, she walks in a garden with Queen Mum (*Round* 72). After he wakes up, he feels lucky to be rejected by the King because "We [they] were now in dire straits for money and I would have looked pretty silly having to borrow from him" (*Round* 72). Including their dreams in the narrative is a reversal of the dominant gravity in classical travel literature and it also adds comic elements when he says they are lucky for his rejecting the offer since they cannot afford such a dinner invitation. It is also comic when he talks about signs: "predicted for me, as a Sagittarian, 'benefits from older people', who would have to get a move on with their generosity or I would be dead; and for Wanda, born under Aries, a glittering future but only if she stayed at home" (*Round* 104). Eric and

Wanda have different predictions for their signs. Considering their advanced age produces the comic effect because Eric is already old, and Wanda does not need to stay at home for a bright future. Therefore, the sense of humour turns the seriousness upside down. The narrative stylistic elements serve as another feature that contributes to the subversion.

Conclusion

Round Ireland in Low Gear (1987) subverts the traditional figure of the explorer-hero in certain ways. Firstly, although the figure of a traditional explorer-hero represents his country's national expansionist ambitions, Eric and Wanda go on this journey only to enjoy and explore a new place. For this aim, they take much more time than they think because their desire to appreciate a spot also intertwines with the desire to convey Eric's observations in detail. The traditional explorer-hero focuses more on the exploration rather than the process of writing. Even if spending more time slows their flow, he makes sure that he spends enough time at each place. Secondly, in his account, Eric can be more subjective because he does not have any sponsor. Because he is financially freer than a traditional figure, his writing is not a promised report. He does not have censorship stemming from the sponsor's wishes. The travel costs him more but it gives chance to apply his comic and ironic tone without being under any obligation. Thirdly, the traditional travel narratives intentionally exclude women because gender norms attribute mobility to men and immobility to women. The entrapment of women in domestic spaces monopolizes the genre under male domination. The travel of Wanda subverts this understanding. Nevertheless, the male representation of the woman traveller remains intricate in the text because she is portrayed as a wife when they need to cook. This is also a textual method to contribute to domesticity. This is reinforced by the fact that biking equipment is considered only for male use. Wanda finds a bicycle for her, yet she has a limited option, unlike Eric who can choose one among the variety of options. Fourthly, although the traditional explorer-hero is a young and virile figure, Eric and Wanda also reverse this notion. Although they are an old age couple on the road, they do not withdraw themselves from travelling as their peers do. Therefore, they also subvert the idea of ageing by culture and challenge this territory. Lastly, travelling as a couple also subverts the traditional understanding of exploration because the conventional heroes are not likely to take their family with them. Companionship has positive and negative sides: either they support each other, or they have quarrels due to the different perspectives on travelling. Constraints are an inevitable part of travel, yet they do not have the urge or aim to overcome all the obstacles like a traditional explorer figure. They do not heroize their actions, which turns them into anti-heroes. This feature is supported through the stylistic elements of irony and comic. The irony is applied to show that they are different from the traditional mighty figure. In this respect, self-criticism operates as a method to show the realities of travelling. As for comic elements, it functions as another device to subvert the seriousness of the traditional accounts. Therefore, Eric and Wanda's travel to Ireland differs from the traditional examples of the genre. While it contributes to the narrative complexity, it also adds a new dimension to the genre.

Bibliography

Bassnett, Susan. "Travel Writing and Gender" *The Cambridge History of Travel Writing.* Ed. Nandini Das and Tim Youngs. Cambridge: Cambridge UP, 2019. 225-242. Print.

Bird, Dunlaith. "Travel Writing and Gender". *The Routledge Companion to Travel Writing.* Ed. Carl Thompson. New York: Routledge, 2016. 81-97. Print.

Das, Nandini. "Early Modern Travel Writing (2): English Travel Writing". *The Cambridge History of Travel Writing.* Ed. Nandini Das and Tim Youngs. Cambridge: Cambridge UP, 2019. 77-93. Print.

Hanbury-Tenison, Robin. *The Oxford Book of Exploration*. Oxford: Oxford UP, 1993. Print.

Hyde, Martin. "Travel and Tourism in Later Life". *The Routledge Handbook of Cultural Gerontology.* Ed. Julia Twigg and Wendy Martin. London: Routledge, 2015. 337-345. Print.

Kinsley, Zoe. "Travellers and Tourists". *The Routledge Companion to Travel Writing.* Ed. Carl Thompson. New York: Routledge, 2016. 382-396. Print.

Meens, Floris and Tom Sintobin. "Who is Carrying the Luggage? Gendered Discourses on Companionship in Travel Writing: An Introduction". *Gender, Companionship and Travel: Discourses in Pre-modern and Modern Travel Literature.* Ed. Floris Meens and Tom Sintobin. London: Routledge, 2019. 11-16. Print.

Newby, Eric. *A Short Walk in the Hindu Kush.* New York: Penguin Books, 1981. Print.

Newby, Eric. *A Traveller's Life.* London: Harper Press, 1982. Print.

Newby, Eric. *Round Ireland in Low Gear*. New York: Viking, 1987. Print.

Pickering, Sam. "Eric Newby and the Literature of Travel". *The Sewanee Review* 115.3 (2007): 479- 483. Print.

Robinson, Jane. *Unsuitable for Ladies: An Anthology of Women Travellers.* Oxford: Oxford UP, 1994. Print.

Sherman, William H. "Stirrings and Searchings (1500-1720)". *The Cambridge Companion to Travel Writing.* Ed. Peter Hulme and Tim Youngs. Cambridge: Cambridge UP, 2002. 17-37. Print.

Smethurst, Paul. "Discovers and Explorers". *The Routledge Companion to Travel Writing.* Ed. Carl Thompson. New York: Routledge, 2016. 366-382. Print.

Thompson, Carl. *Travel Writing*. London: Routledge, 2011. Print.

Thubron, Colin. "Travel Writing Today". *Travel Writing: Critical Concepts in Literary and Cultural Studies*. Ed. Charles Forsdick and Tim Youngs. Vol 1, London: Routledge, 2012. Print.

A Short Bio of Res. Assist. Elif DEMİR

Elif Demir earned her Ph.D. from the department of English Language and Literature at Ankara University. She works as a Research Assistant at Sivas Cumhuriyet University. Her research interests cover literary theories and the representations of body and gender in 21st century English novels.